THE MEDIEVAL TOWN

JOHN H. MUNDY

Professor of History
Columbia University

AND

PETER RIESENBERG

Professor of History
Washington University

AN ANVIL ORIGINAL
under the general editorship of
LOUIS L. SNYDER

VAN NOSTRAND REINHOLD COMPANY
NEW YORK, CINCINNATI
TORONTO   LONDON
MELBOURNE

To

RICHARD WILDER EMERY

one who gives
knowledge to many
virtue to all

Van Nostrand Reinhold Company Regional Offices:
Cincinnati   New York   Chicago   Millbrae   Dallas

Van Nostrand Reinhold Company Foreign Offices:
London   Toronto   Melbourne

Copyright © 1958 by John H. Mundy and Peter Riesenberg

Library of Congress Catalog Card Number: 58-8608

All rights reserved. No part of this work covered by the copyright hereon may be reproduced or used in any form or by any means—graphic, electronic, or mechanical, including photocopying, recording, taping, or information storage and retrieval systems—without written permission of the publisher. Manufactured in the United States of America.

Published by Van Nostrand Reinhold Company
450 West 33rd Street, New York, N.Y. 10001

Published simultaneously in Canada by
D. Van Nostrand Company (Canada), Ltd.

15 14 13 12 11 10 9

PREFACE

The history of the medieval town is the concern of this essay and collection of documents. We intend to present a rounded picture of town life and institutions in as brief a compass as possible. Aspects of urban education, religion, and mores are integrated into this treatment. Constitutional history is treated from the political and juridical sides as well as from that of the history of social groups and classes. Economic history is placed in the contexts of the relationship of town and countryside and of the general evolution of commerce and industry.

Many problems confront the epitomizer of medieval town history. An obvious one is the size of the topic. This study concerns western urbanism: Arabic and Byzantine cities are mentioned only as background. We seek also to avoid the usual concentration upon materials drawn from northern Europe. Due weight is given to Italy and the Mediterranean. Moreover, we are aware that the past has heard scholarly arguments on every issue in medieval urban history. While recording the principal opinions, we do not see our task as that of the historiographer. We are principally interested in the medieval town and its inhabitants, not in the historians of its institutions.

We have divided our task. Mr. Mundy wrote the historical essay; Mr. Riesenberg prepared the documents. We have worked together happily and sometimes humorously.

Mr. Mundy wishes to thank the Columbia University Council for Research in the Social Sciences and the Social Science Research Council for their aid to his studies of urban history. The authors also wish to thank Mr. Donald R. Kelley for his aid with the index.

January, 1958   JOHN H. MUNDY

                                   PETER RIESENBERG

TABLE OF CONTENTS

Part One

MEDIEVAL URBANISM

— 1 —

A DEFINITION OF URBANISM

A town is a relatively permanent concentration of men and their habitations. So also is a village. We distinguish between a town and a village by stating that the former is rather larger than the latter. In the medieval period, the village was nearer in size than the town to the median or average agglomeration of men and their habitations.

This definition is deficient in several ways. First, it is too relative. In terms of size, what was a town in the middle ages is today a mere village. What was a village in the middle ages was a town in prehistoric times. On the other hand, because a term has a history or tradition, our definition is too arbitrary. Who thinks of a town and a village as essentially the same? Yet that is what we wish to say for the moment. There is no real dividing line between a town and a village. Both are concentrations of men and their habitations, and they differ only in size. This is, however, the advantage of our definition. It reminds us that there is no absolute difference between town and country, between urban society and rural. What the historian of urbanism records is simply a changing relationship of concentration and emptiness: a pattern characteristic of man's social life throughout the ages. While, therefore, this essay deals only with the town in medieval Europe, our definition relates it to the life of all men at all times.

Because men live together for many purposes, towns serve many functions. Before describing these, however, we must remind ourselves that the development of these functions is dependent upon the technological state of a given society at a specific time. Indeed, it is obvious that permanent and sizable concentrations of men were not possible before the late neolithic revolutions in agrarian techniques. In a more limited sense, also, technology plays a part in developing towns and choosing their sites. During the middle ages, Dinant and Liège were industrial centers because of nearby mineral deposits. In general, then, urbanism can exist only when man's means of exploiting nature have reached a certain stage, and will flourish only in regions endowed with fertile soil or other natural gifts. There are no great towns in barren wastes on the way to nowhere. Viewed from the purely technological or economic aspect, towns are analogous to plants and vegetables that grow where the soil is rich.

Town Functions. The first function and most energy-consuming part of town life is therefore work or industry: the means by which man aliments himself from nature. But man is not simply a vegetable, specialized in the utilization of nature external to himself. To use it efficaciously, man must regulate his relations with other men. For use or abuse, to each individual man, other men are part of nature. With this amplification, we may say that man's relationship to nature is also expressed in the myriad institutions conventionally grouped under the terms of commerce, government, and religion. These are the principal functions served by urbanism.

Evolved societies specialize, and this is reflected in urban form. Although commerce, government, and religion are found in every town, specialization causes one or another of these functions to predominate. Of these, the religious or the ideological is rarely found isolated, as a dominant characteristic. This is because ideology, like the alchemist's mercury, has the capacity to inform and endow all other functions. In the middle ages, however, some towns came close to embodying and living off the ideological function. Rome was an outstanding example. Insignificant as a commercial center, it was not even the capital of a large secular state. It was the capital of the ecclesiastical administration of Latin Christendom. Admittedly, the clergy have no monopoly of religion or ideology and are not necessarily to be confused with it. That Rome's ecclesiastical role was connected to a religious one, however, is evidenced by a fact that determined its medieval political and social life: pilgrimage. Pilgrimage or ecclesiastical tourism had much to do with religion. To Rome went doubter, believer, and curious alike to touch the main symbols of a common civilization.

Predominance of a town by government is easier to exemplify. Rome grew rapidly during the late Republic. Its enlargement was principally evoked by the fact that the Republic was summoned to rule the Mediterranean. Government, however, is not only administration. One of its principal aspects is military: concentration for defense or attack. During and after the anarchy of the third century after Christ, the military element in Mediterranean and Roman urbanism became increasingly prominent. The weight of town life shifted toward the *limes,* the military frontier. The spread of the *limes* in this and the later age of invasion created a pattern of militarized urbanism that indelibly marked the medieval town. Henry Sumner Maine told us that medieval institutions derived partly from the generalization of the *limes* throughout the whole of Europe.[1] And his insight is authenticated by the names which medieval men often used to describe their towns and villages: *castra* and *castella.*

There is little need to emphasize the functions of commerce and industry. Labor and bartering are obviously necessary for town life, and many communities were dominated by them. In the middle ages, Milan was a center of industry, Genoa of maritime trade. Indeed, it sometimes seems that business and industry were so universal that they outweighed all other functions. Men rarely went to war, and even more seldom to religion. But this fact can be overemphasized. Men sleep more than they make love. But, did sleep determine it, bedrooms would have no walls, and poets and jurists alike would do little but yawn. By itself, frequency is not a primary gauge of significance. While the market place was characteristic of the medieval town, urban architecture was dominated by the towers of church, battlement, and administrative palaces.

Communication. Our definition of urbanism has so far concentrated on only two aspects: on the town as

[1] See the Bibliography for the appropriate work of this author and for those of other important authors mentioned from time to time in this essay.

a concentration of men and habitations, and on the delineation of the principal functions performed there. What is needed is a factor that relates concentration to the successful performance of function. This factor is communication. A town is almost always located at the hub of a communication network. Almost always, we say, because geographical endowment and historical tradition play a role in determining town location. Towns can be built and last for generations simply to exploit a mine. Generally, however, such towns are rare and relatively transitory. Specific illustrations will balance our view and underline the significance of communication.

Medieval Rome was primarily a religious center. It was not particularly easy of access. Pilgrimage and church administration could have been better served by location at Avignon or Genoa. That Rome was the medieval capital of Latin Europe, therefore, testifies to the importance of tradition. Nevertheless, common sense reminds us that Rome was not built on Spitzbergen ice nor the sands of Timbuctoo. Its religious function, in short, was aided by the fact that Rome was on communication routes.

Governmental and military functions are also served by communication. Here again, however, particular needs place towns at sites that are not rational purely from the point of view of communication. Tuscan or Provençal medieval hilltop towns show that the best defense is not always found down in the valley, near highway or navigable stream. In general, however, administration and defense are best served by a town near the center of the region to be governed. By center, of course, we mean nothing mechanical. As in the medieval principality of Salzburg, geography often places the natural center of a province toward the political frontier. Moreover, military necessity is not always best served by central defense. Paris became the capital of France during the Scandinavian invasions up the Seine river during the ninth century. Its history shows the importance of locating a center of defense hard against the frontier.

As for commerce, its dependence upon routes of communication is so obvious as to need no underlining. Even primarily industrial urbanism was centered near convenient transport facilities in the middle ages. The principal nucleus of town life and industry in north Europe lay along the Atlantic coast upon the waterways lying between the Rhine and Loire rivers. On occasion, also, the type of facility needed for commerce changed the localities in which towns flourished. To paraphrase Henri Pirenne, the end of the barbarian invasions and the rise of commerce in the eleventh century brought the town down from the hilltop into the valley.

The Townsman. We have claimed that there was no distinction in kind between a town and a village. Because a burgher is obviously not like a peasant, however, there must be a distinction of some sort. The difference is a matter of degree: the town is a more intense concentration of men and housing than the village. And it is a more active center of communication.

Concentration has advantages and disadvantages. The medieval town defended itself better than the village but was more threatened by fire and disease. In all ages, townsmen lack living space. In twelfth century Toulouse, the new rich moved to the bourg outside of the city's walls. They built spaciously there, and looked back without regret to the cramped quarters of the older center. To avoid the heat, burghers preferred to spend August in the country. On the other hand, nearby country gentlemen habitually spent winter in town. Due to concentration, also, land is in relatively short supply in town. Because the economic utilization of land obliges the farmer to live reasonably near his fields, farming cannot be the primary enterprise of town inhabitants. True, many burgher fortunes were made in land speculation and agrarian enterprise during the middle ages. Moreover, ownership and operation of small fields and farms by townsmen was much more significant in the little medieval town than it is today. But the basic definition of the medieval town is that most of its citizens did not make their living by working in the fields.

This fact caused townsmen hardship. Their food and raw materials were in the hands of foreigners, the countryfolk. The burghers' advantages, however, were correspondingly great because their specialties were naturally those to which the villager could devote little time. We need not stress how a relatively large group of townsmen engaged in the same industry developed techniques superior to those of isolated village artisans. It was not in villages that Peter of Montreuil and Villard of Honnecourt learned the architecture they transplanted from France to Germany, Hungary, and Cyprus in the thirteenth century. Obviously, however, the degree of specialization was not as high in the middle ages as today. Village industry was always significant. In northern Europe, for example, tableware was usually wood, manufactured by peasants during the winter.

Another equally important urban superiority was the technique of business that naturally flourished among those who had the advantage of living at the hub of a communication network. Townsmen were better than farmers at trafficking, arranging for transportation, and handling money. Implementing these were superior legal methods and documentation of property and business. Moreover, the town was the center of intellectual life. The great jurist Bartolus did not remain long in his native Sassoferrato. He taught in Bologna and Perugia. The church was centered in the towns. It was there that the cathedrals were built. In spite of the monks' desire to flee pullulating humanity, the most famous monasteries of the thirteenth century were located within or adjacent to towns. The principal centers of learning were there: the cathedral schools, the Dominican *studia,* the universities. Even the nobility, so much of whose power was derived from properties and fastnessess outside of towns, were never more noble than when residing or visiting there. Christian of Troyes, the great twelfth century poet of chivalry, had his hero Erec fight his first tourney in one town and his last duel in another.

Concentration and communication explain the intellectual superiority of the town. Men jostled each other more there. They traveled more and saw more foreigners. Their view was ampler. They talked more. In 1202, the burghers of Tournus petitioned their Burgundian lord to abolish his rights over marriage. Like peasants, they sought freedom from control and taxes. But they also appealed because foreigners passing through town mocked the good citizens, calling them serfs. Now all men seek the advantages that they see others to have, but, unlike peasants, medieval townsmen saw more of what others had.

These remarks imply, however, no fundamental distinction between townsman and countryman. Excluding high intellectual or mechanical specialties, the techniques of urban living were—and still are—easy to acquire. Medieval peasants who had come to town not infrequently gained huge fortunes. Again, urban man has no monopoly upon invention. First, rural society has its own specialties and invents for them. Second, there are moments in the relationship of town and country when villagers seem to step ahead. Though rarer than its opposite, this process has often been evidenced in history and is most noticeable when an economy or society decentralizes. Although the late Roman town was not uninventive, the formation of a new society was the creation of the countryside. Industry went rural, as it were, and the great innovation of late Rome was the change in the utilization of land and the erection of the domanial system.

These observations indicate that there is another side to urbanism than simply the history of the town itself. This side is the relationship of the town to the countryside. By virtue of being relatively large concentrations and centers of communication, towns specialize in techniques differing from those of the countryside. The pattern of different specializations makes for a certain harmony between town and village. The town has industrial and intellectual products to offer in exchange for food and raw materials. Man's commerce is always fraught with difficulties, however, and where we posit mutual need, we are sure to find mutual hostility. The town endeavors to sell its services at maximum price and the village to exploit town needs. A conflict of interests is a necessary expression of town-country relations.

— 2 —

ORIGINS OF THE MEDIEVAL TOWN

The basic institutional endowment of medieval Europe came from the Mediterranean. Admittedly, even during Rome's greatest periods, significant cultures lay north of the Rhine and Danube frontier. But these northern and largely German civilizations were primitive. Up to the third century A.D., the Germans were tribal in political organization, economically almost nomadic, materially ill-equipped, and relatively few in numbers. It is, therefore, in the Mediterranean that we perceive the principal origins of medieval town life.

Latin and Greek civilization under the aegis of Rome underwent a profound crisis during the third century A.D. From Syria to Britain, provincials sought and attained equality with the original Italic and Roman people. Related to this was a change in the economy of the Latin provinces from the first century A.D. to the fourth and fifth. Reaching a height by the third century, the provinces learned from their erstwhile master and emancipated themselves from dependence upon Italic and Roman industry and direction. This started a process of diffusion that continued through the German invasions and the early middle ages until Scandinavia and even Iceland lay within a diluted but still Latin culture.

Future glories aside, this process brought difficulties. Second and third century provincial growth resulted in the enhancement of local industry for domestic markets. As Michael Rostovtzeff has shown, however, the higher industrial and commercial techniques of the older Mediterranean withered in the unpropitious atmosphere of an increasingly localist economy. As the periphery rose, the center sank, and, by the late empire, even the Germans beyond the frontier had nearly attained technological parity with the Mediterranean. Indeed, the rise of the provinces imperilled Rome itself. Pushed out of provincial markets, shorn of administrative and even ideological leadership, Rome, as the symbol of the old central regions, became only a swollen parasite. Though its dismantling was already underway, generations passed before it was accomplished. In the meantime, Rome's crisis siphoned back creative energies from the new provinces. The Latin tradition of *Romanitas* was the school for the provincials; but the tuition fees were exorbitant.

The third century presaged the course of the future. Barbarian invasions and the creation of permanent political institutions among the Germans demonstrated that imperial provinces were not the only beneficiaries of the spread of Mediterranean civilization. More significant was the collapse of Mediterranean unity. Drained of youth and energy, the provinces defended themselves but separated from the family of *Romanitas*. For nine years, Gaul, Britain, and Spain split off from Rome. For fifteen years, the near eastern domains seceded, creating a prophetic Helleno-Arabic state. Moreover, prices rose catastrophically, endangering the alimentation of the army and civil government. Localist economy produced for local need, but Rome's unity required export production.

The Late Roman State. Mediterranean unity survived the half century crisis by building a new society. Before the breakdown, the state had existed beyond society, as it were, simply to maintain peace and defend the frontiers. Only in a few centers had it designedly served deeper social functions. During and after the crisis, however, it entered into society, endeavoring to construct a world both perfect and predictable. The fact that this state eventually failed does not permit us to despise its attainments. Its might lasted long—throughout the fourth century—and its inheritance was enormous.

Initially, the new design was to feed the army and civil administration. This function was performed in two ways. The first was by direct state management, as of the armaments industry. The second way involved the state in the more significant task of mobilizing the whole society. To aliment itself predictably, the state regulated prices and reformed the tax system to make it more responsive to economic actuality. The municipalities also were called upon for service. Their well-to-do citizens or *curiales* were charged with administrative tasks and held responsible for the imperial taxes levied on the town and its region. In return, the towns were actively aided. The imperial government subsidized public building. The results of this policy were to be seen in stylistic innovation, such as the Constantinian basilica, and also in the founding of the new Rome at Constantinople. In addition, all principal industrial and commercial specialties were brigaded into *collegia* endowed with duties and corresponding privileges. Indeed, all society was eventually organized into functional orders serving the commonwealth.

The ordering of society into functional orders created

a new social structure and laid the foundations for the middle ages. Each social order possessed duties, privileges, and special jurisdictions to implement its work. The idea that each group has its own law, therefore, was not a German innovation; it was the essence of late Rome's social orders. Moreover, the old classical conception of liberty was replaced by something less grand but more socially exact. Gildsmen, or *collegiati,* were privileged, for example, even to the equestrian grade. But privilege depended upon obligatory service. This perception of an inmixture of liberty and servitude pervaded late Roman and much of medieval social thought.

The emphasis upon service to the common good, moreover, inspired a general ethical program of social renovation. The admission of lesser social elements into the senatorial and equestrian orders during the late third and early fourth centuries attests a desire to attain a closer coincidence than had prevailed before between reward or privilege and service to the commonwealth. Accent was put on public gain and not on private profit. From Constantine on, the church aided the state by legislating and declaiming against usury, as at Nicea in 325. The state's wide social scope is seen in 370, when the doctors of Constantinople were instructed to supervise the grain distribution and urged "rather honestly to serve the poor than dishonestly the rich."

In spite of temporary success, however, the history of urbanism in the western provinces of the empire shows us that economic decentralization and provincial separatism continued despite all efforts. True, a few military and governmental centers, such as Trier and Milan, attained new heights. But Rome sank throughout the fourth century, and the average town continued to weaken. Autun shrank from a town of five hundred acres to a village of twenty-five. Moreover, the countryside was splitting off from the town. When the empire became Christian, the townsmen readily converted. The peasants, or *pagani,* resisted. Again, the insecurities of a warlike age obliged towns to fortify themselves and rendered useless the aqueducts with which they once reached far out into the countryside to slake their thirst.

Within each province, resistance to imperial authority was necessarily expressed by the hostility of the *pagani* to

the officials and tax collectors who came from the municipalities. Veritable assassins of towns, the endemic Gallic
Bagaudae or African *Circoncelliones* were peasant rebels
and bandits. Still more important was the alliance of
villagers and great notables against the towns. The magnates held important state offices or were the heirs of
officers, and were, therefore, in a position to brake the
exploitation of the *pagani* by municipal officialdom. Moreover, their wealth endowed both the villagers and their
own growing estates with *gynecea,* or slave workshops,
that produced an increasing percentage of the industrial
goods once bought or made in towns. This was not the
only time in Europe's history that great landlords and
peasant banditti together eviscerated an urbanism.

Faced by continuing responsibility to the state and
mounting rural hostility, the municipalities withered and
the order of the *curiales* all but vanished. As urban industry collapsed, the businessman was replaced by the
itinerant merchant or peddler. Despised and dangerous,
a shrinking commerce attracted ever fewer local recruits.
Dealing in slaves and luxuries for landed magnates and
high officers of state and church, foreigners, notably
Syrians and Jews, were becoming the commercial caste
of the west by the time of the German invasions.

In short, the new order of the late Roman state was not
able to arrest the secession of the provinces or the general
disintegration of Mediterranean society. In its efforts to
prevent this process, it was obliged to make coercive
what had before been voluntary. The division of society
into functional social groups became a system of quasi-
hereditary orders. Privilege and distinctions of dress were
not enough to make men do their duty. Some, such as
minters, were bound as slaves and their costume became
a brand applied with the hot iron. In this age marked by
increasing police power and coercion, it became the good
man's duty to resist. From the days of Theodosius, the
Mediterranean empire slowly fell apart.

The Invasions. Rome's disintegration was com-
pleted by barbarian invasions. Every frontier produced
immigrants, from Ireland's Celts to the Saharan tribes. The
first large settlements were those of the Germans, fleeing
the Huns of the eastern steppe in the fourth century.
While the great period was the fifth century, lesser German

movements continued in the sixth. Islam appeared in the seventh century, and its incursions into the Near East, Africa, and Spain continued into the eighth. After the Germans, north and east Europe was still not quiet. The Slaves settled the Balkans and peopled eastern Europe and Russia north of the steppe during the seventh century. The ninth and tenth centuries witnessed the last major movements. The Scandinavians, the Magyar steppe-folk, and a final Moslem push further reduced the areas of Hellenic and Latin culture.

For a moment, we pause at 800 A.D., the year when Charlemagne reconstituted the Latin empire. The invasions had been destructive. The Slavs and steppe-folk had erased Latin culture and town life in the Balkans. The western invasions had not been so severe. The first intruders, Goths and Franks, sought to preserve Rome's urban society. Later waves, such as that of the Lombards, had wreaked more damage, obliterating the towns along the upper Danubian frontier. Initially, also, Islamic society was vigorously anti-urban, implementing, for example, rural hostility to Alexandria and Carthage whose ports drew off the *annona*, or grain, to Rome and Constantinople.

Destruction, however, is not the only aspect of the invasions worth recording. The invasions split the Mediterranean into three principal blocs, typified by language: Latin, Greek, and Arabic. At least until the twelfth century, the last of these was the greatest. While the Moslems destroyed much of Mediterranean town life, they speedily reconstructed it. A new and lively urbanism—Cordova, Kairouan, Cairo, Damascus, and Baghdad—grew rapidly from the time of the conquest and reached its peak during the eighth and ninth centuries. (*See Document No. 1.*) Mixed with Iranian and Mesopotamian elements, moreover, a transmuted Mediterranean civilization eventually spread from the Near East to Africa, India and the Pacific, to Sumatra and beyond. Islam marked a turning point in the relationship of the eastern Mediterranean to its near eastern neighbors. The choice of Damascus as against Antioch for the Omayyad capital signaled a new direction: the Islamic Mediterranean looked eastward.

The rise of Islamic urbanism at first boded ill for Latin Europe. The Syrian merchants disappeared, finding better business to the east. Absorbing Egypt, Africa, and eventually Sicily, the Moslems were free of the need to import grain. The west had little industry to offer them. Senegal and the Sudan, the two gold producing regions, fell into their hands. The west, therefore, had only one principal commodity to sell: man power, slaves for palace military elites and labor. Implying a condition not unlike that of Africa in the eighteenth century, this trade was unhappy indeed. But its importance for the European town may not be underestimated. Islam's rapid rise stimulated the whole Mediterranean basin.

The second great power was Byzantium. Until the thirteenth century, Constantinople was by far the greatest city in Christian hands. (*See Document No. 3.*) Byzantine hegemony in the western Mediterranean, also, died only slowly, leaving lasting traces on western institutions. The coasts and islands were Byzantine until well into the eighth century; Venice remained her dominion until the tenth century, and southern Italy until the latter half of the eleventh. The law schools of Ravenna, Rome, and even later Bologna would have been inconceivable without Byzantium. The Greeks, however, were not limited to giving only death bed instruction. The Slavs in the Balkans and Russia accepted their culture and religion, and modeled their nascent towns upon what they saw on the Bosphorus.

Least of the three cultural segments was that of the Latins and their German rulers. The German kings who divided the western empire tried to continue Rome's traditions. Roman edicts were received and published until the sixth century, and even Justinian's later legislation influenced the west through the church. But the whole structure was subtly simplified and altered. One aspect of this change is shown by the history of social orders. By the ninth century, the elaborate and articulated social and functional groups of late Roman law had been reduced to three grand orders: the clergy, the soldiers or knights (*milites*), and the laborers. As in Rome, emphasis was placed upon function and service: we pray for you, we fight for you, and, to use the old Frisian joke, we lay eggs for you. The two commanding orders, the clergy and soldiery, derived their traditions and characteristics from somewhat different sources. Whether introduced into Mediterranean society as conquerors or as soldiers in Rome's service, the Germans everywhere reinvigorated the heroic virtues of those who wear the sword. From the age of the invasions, a diluted cultural Germanism or rather a stalwart if sometimes self-conscious primitivism became the distinguishing mark of the medieval military aristocracy, regardless of its particular racial or cultural origins.

The clergy, on the other hand, were the heirs and the refuge of *Romanitas* and of its traditions of literacy and learning. In France, for example, the vast majority of the higher clergy was of provincial or Latin origin well into the seventh century. The results of this was that literacy, and hence knowledge of jurisprudence, became the monopoly of the western ecclesiastical order, except in those regions still ruled or directly influenced by the Byzantines. By the time of Charlemagne, the western state machinery was half ecclesiastic and half lay. Let there be no mistake: secular power still dominated, and Charlemagne ruled both church and state. That the clergy were already moving toward leadership, however, is clear. On the restoration of the western empire in 800 A.D., the definition of Europe was essentially ecclesiastical. Its religion separated it from Islam; Latin, its ecclesiastical language, from the Byzantines.

The Early Western Town. These changes meant much for town life. The splitting of the Mediterranean in the fifth through the beginning of the ninth centuries encouraged the gradual simplification or reduction of urban institutions. By Charlemagne's time, our main evidence of significant industry is the export prohibition of weapons to the barbarians of the north. Gallic artisan *collegia* disappeared by the end of the sixth century and we may only presume a measure of continuity in the greater Italian towns. Of course, the artisan's function had not been lost. It had come to rest in the quasi-servile *gynecea* or village industry. Moreover, commerce continued declining and was surrendered to foreigners. In France, Syrians imported luxuries until into the eighth century. After their departure, only the tenacious merchants of Jewry acted as intermediaries between the Moslems and Christians. Slaves became the principal export to the Mediterranean. This traffic was among the reasons for the Carolingian militarism that unified the west by 800 A.D. The reconquest of southern France by Charles Martel, the wars of Charlemagne against the Saxons and Avars, all harvested men for the marts of the inland sea. The Slavs were the particular objects of western enterprise and finally gave their name to the institution in which they were bound.

The administrative functions of the town also underwent simplification. Having first experienced town life along the Roman military frontier, the German kings combined civil and military administration under counts appointed to govern each old Roman *civitas,* or city.[2] This served to continue the town as administrative capital of the area about its walls. On the other hand, it reduced the revenue that went to town purposes and diminished the already weakened electoral autonomy of late Roman times. Even the attempt of Charlemagne to insist that townsmen elect their *scabini* or assessor-judges and notaries did little more for the moment than underline the decline of old institutions. The town also continued to lose direct control of the countryside. Town counts were obliged to treat rural areas as quasi-independent and to separate the rural courts of the hundreds or the vicarages from that in the town.

Furthermore, the bishops began to play an increasing role in town administration. Elected by clergy and people of the town alone, they soon assumed an effective presidency. While their power was sometimes only informal, it was often recognized by a grant of comital grade or of immunity from the ordinary royal administration. It thus came about that the bishop and his lay and clerical court were the true heirs of the civil as against the military tradition of Roman urbanism. As the system of registering documents in town archives before the town fathers

[2] In this essay, the word *city* is used to translate the term *civitas.* There is only one rare exception to this rule. City is sometimes employed to describe the great city, or megalopolis, of ancient and modern times. Our usage has a historical justification. In most of Europe until the thirteenth century, *civitates* were usually towns founded in the Roman epoch. Because we wish to stress the distinction between old and new urbanism, our convention seems useful.

and notaries slowly collapsed, the clergy began to assume these functions also. Even in Italy, most ninth century scribes were clerks. In the north, the church monopolized the documentation of property right. Although the church provided continuity with the classic past, the secular urban culture of Rome had all but disappeared.

In spite of atrophy, several progressive trends may be seen in town life during this long period. The decline was not consistent and there were even several brief periods of growth. During much of the sixth and seventh centuries and again during the late eighth and early ninth, Frankish success and maintenance of the peace encouraged towns to grow a little. By the latter ninth century, Cologne boasted six churches, other than its cathedral: three were of Roman origin, two Merovingian, and one Carolingian. While this statistic shows increase, it also indicates that each period of growth was less significant than the one before. When the Scandinavians overran it in 882, Trier was a small settlement huddled in a corner of the Roman walled enclosure.

Occasional reprieves from extinction, however, are not the whole story. Frankland was a northern power, centered in the Rhine and Meuse valleys. It was the first new state to lie beyond as well as within Rome's frontiers, and it witnessed the first signs of northern Europe's awakening. While the Mediterranean languished, the Franks and Frisians turned toward the north. Charlemagne's main toll stations lay on rivers flowing into the North Sea and the Channel. His commercial regulations dealt with export trade to the north. Butter and parchment replaced Mediterranean olive oil and papyrus in the Carolingian empire. While we may not yet speak of northern urbanism, the shift of civilization was underway.

Unfortunately for the west, the future was not so bright as Charlemagne's reign seemed to promise. Aided by the forgetfulness of peaceful years, the separatism that was part of the Roman inheritance moved provinces, the clergy and magnates, to minimize royal power. The new west again began to split up. Scandinavians, Saracens, Hungarians, and even Slavs profited from this disintegration to raid and desolate Europe during the ninth and tenth centuries. There was need in their attacks: the Moslems sought slaves and the Norse ironware and weapons. The past militarism of the Franks, moreover, had educated their enemies. The vigorous Magyars had replaced the enslaved Avars in Hungary. Seeking gold and slaves, they raided as far as Rheims and Nîmes. From 826, also, the entry of Frankish Christianity into the Scandinavian north emphasized the power of the Christian king and thus dispossessed the old pagen sacred nobilities. These now led a Norse emigration against Latin Europe.

The immediate results of these incursions was catastrophic. Northern Europe's tender new urbanism was all but obliterated. Further south, Saracen raids almost cut France off from Italy. Sanctuaries and towns were plundered of wealth accumulated in long years of peace. Arles retired within the walls of its Roman arena. Some towns, such as Frejus, entirely disappeared. Only inland areas, Lombardy, central France, and western Germany escaped the full weight of the assault. Economists have often underlined the mercantile aspect of these raids: those who came to plunder stayed to trade. But plundering came first. After the gold and iron had been taken, the Norse could still find a thing of value: the slave. However ebullient, it is hard to barter when one is oneself a prime commodity.

From hindsight, we know that the barbarians and Saracens were bound to be repulsed. True, a peripheral culture, that of Ireland, was ruined forever. But the Scandinavians were able to effect only two permanent landings: one fairly large in England, and another small enclave at the mouth of the Seine. The Magyars left even less of an impress. Indeed, these peoples were too backward and too few in number to smash western civilization. While much more advanced, the Moslems did not exert their full strength. Nor does it seem likely that North Africa and Spain were mighty enough to overthrow their northern neighbor.

As we have seen, furthermore, the Norse emigrations were partly an aspect of the spread of Latin Christianity. By their end, all of Europe had become Christian. During their movements, the Norse linked together the Atlantic and the eastern Mediterranean. From Greenland, their reach extended to Constantinople. Scandinavian warrior merchants dotted Baltic islands and shores and Russia's rivers with trading posts. Although some later suffered eclipse, many, such as Kiev and Novgorod, became the capitals of regional states as the invaders and indigenes fused together. In short, the end of this cycle of invasions saw Europe surrounded by settled states centered in primitive but important urban settlements. These states were certainly capable of warfare but had lost the migratory characteristics of barbarian society. Barbarism had been expelled from Europe.

— 3 —

THE RISE OF THE MEDIEVAL TOWN

Although there are evidences as early as the ninth century for Italy, the Latin west generally began to grow again during the tenth century. From that time, Europe rose, slowly at first and then more rapidly in the eleventh and twelfth centuries. The most obvious evidence is the growth of population, of the area under tillage, and of towns. So impressive was the increase in human fecundity that it itself has been described as the reason for Europe's upswing.

Dependent upon psychological and practical factors, however, population increase cannot be used to explain itself. Historians have therefore looked elsewhere for the cause of Europe's advance. Henri Pirenne underlined the importance of outside stimuli. The Norse brought Byzantine gold and other commodities into the Baltic and North Sea, for example, thereby enlivening industry and trade in Flanders, England, and Germany. More consequent was the rise of Italian maritime traffic with the eastern Mediterranean at the time of Byzantine greatness in the ninth and tenth centuries. Venetians and Amalfitans sold slaves to Islam and brought back Byzantine luxuries to Europe. (*See Document No. 2.*)

The significance of external stimulus may not be denied. Like other men, the European emulated his betters. Our second chapter pointed out how Byzantine institutions served as models for later Italian ones. Islamic influence was equally weighty, giving the west much of its maritime technique and business language. The words "admiral" and "risk" are of Arabic origin. But when all has been admitted, it is wise to evaluate the foreign contribution modestly. Foreigners provide markets and education, but these do not themselves equip man to exploit or to learn. Western seaports need not have been bases for native merchants, home from Alexandria or Constantinople. As before, they might have been harbors for foreign slave hunters and exploiters. A port is not only a way out; it is also a way in.

While useful, therefore, the theory of external stimulus does not suffice to explain the rise of European commerce. Other reasons for this phenomenon must be sought in Europe's internal development. Historians have often lamented the decentralizing or feudalizing of civil and military power that marked this age. But there were advantages to this process. The downward passage of political power filled Europe with fortified centers of local resistance. Marches such as Catalonia and Flanders were designed for defense. But it was not so much the fortifications themselves as it was the reinvigoration of western community and cultural solidarity. The developing institution of vassalage linked together the military aristocracy. More, the devolution of political and social command engendered a community sense that bound the inhabitants of the seignory or larger castellany to their lord, their chief in war and peace. By the eleventh century, Europe possessed an interlocking system of defense in depth.

A capacity to defend oneself establishes a sort of peace, but is insufficient in itself. Within each society, individuals seek their advantage beyond the frontiers or, if repressed, at the cost of community harmony. A healthy society builds agencies to capitalize and direct outward this lively aggressiveness. Capitalization requires an assembly of goods, money, and technical personnel that a decentralized economy lacks. Seignors and towns had land or basic techniques but they lacked means of mobilization. The eleventh century counts of Flanders, for example, stimulated town and country alike by building fortified bourgs and by draining marshes. But the scope of their efforts was purely regional.

The church, however, had a broader reach than any secular prince. In the towns, the bishops aided princes to foster a simplified version of late Roman economic regulation, reminding men of the services they owed the community. Although rarely effectively prohibited, usury was frowned upon, thereby steering investors away from the immediate profits of luxury and consumer credit into more basic enterprise. In short, a provident and traditional police protected the first growth of Europe's economy. But the church had a still more positive role to play. While the secular clergy was essentially local or regional, Europe-wide monastic orders arose from the tenth century. Primarily agrarian, these orders were able to mobilize ample resources for great purposes. Throughout the eleventh and twelfth centuries, the monks invested in land mortgages. Capital was dear in those early days, but land was plentiful and barely settled. But the primary activity of the clergy was not, nor could ever be, lending money. The monks usually worked in partnership with secular or ecclesiastical lords to develop lands and capitalize exploitations. These partnerships had implications that transcend economics. They were instrumental in creating the feudal seignory or castellany.

The economic activity of the monastic orders in France, for example, may be divided into different ages. The initial one was that of Cluny in the tenth and eleventh centuries. This militant order either introduced its mission into old monasteries or built new ones in already inhabited centers. It was, therefore, active both in town and country. For a moment in the late eleventh century, for example, all the parish churches of Toulouse were associated with Cluny, save those attached directly to the cathedral, itself recently reformed by this order. As the first revival, Cluny naturally worked within the framework of the old.

At the end of the eleventh and the beginning of the twelfth century, a second and vastly greater stage of monastic work began. One of many, the Cistercian order alone outdistanced Cluny. The new orders worked everywhere, in old communities and out. Typical of the age, the Cistercians and Carthusians went beyond the frontiers of settled society to make deserts into gardens. The scale of enterprise was tremendous. In partnership with local lords, the Hospitallers alone created and settled forty villages near Muret on the Garonne river in an area twenty-five by twelve miles between 1100 and 1110. With modifications, what was true of France was true of all Europe. What the monks had begun, others continued. The great primeval forest belt of the northern European plain was broken into. The clearing of river valleys not only gave new soil to the plough but also opened the rivers for transportation. The internal frontiers of Europe expanded everywhere.

Gaining presidency from the decentralization of secular political power, from the leadership exercised by the clergy and particularly the monks, a revived papacy rose to command Europe's expansion in the eleventh and twelfth centuries. The papal role was imperial. Diocletian had fought to preserve *Romanitas*. Charlemagne battled to convert the Saxons. The popes now summoned the westerners to make the world safe for Latin Christianity. Blessed by the pope, the French conquered England in 1066. The Saracens suffered Holy War in Spain. The Pisans and Genoese conquered the Tyrrhenian sea and raided Tunisia with papal aid. The Latins conquered Sicily as fiefholders of St. Peter. In 1095, the first Crusade to the Holy Land was launched. With the Crusade came the creation of military and financial agencies to hold and extend Latin power in the Near East.

The connection with commerce is obvious. The Crusades were part of the opening of the Mediterranean to European maritime and commercial enterprise. What is less evident is how the church, an agency devoted to peace and charity, could lead an imperialism. But peace is not so far from war as we sometimes hope. The idea of the Crusade was closely affiliated with that of the Peace of God. The venom drawn from the body social was used to good effect outside. Nobles, merchants, and even the poor swept the Moslems and Byzantines alike from the high seas. The Mediterranean almost became a Latin lake from about 1150 to 1350. In short, the oecumenical church provided the leadership and capitalization that lifted a localist and partly autarkic society out of itself and sent it forward into the world about it.

The Town. It was in this circumstance that the Latin town rose again. The earliest signs of the new age of urban history were in the ninth and particularly the tenth centuries. First touched were the areas that profited from outside stimulus: Venice and southern Italy, and, to a lesser degree, the northern coasts of the German empire. The first evidences of growth seem petty and occasional; they were efforts to rehabilitate, not really to expand. The real expansion began during the eleventh and twelfth centuries. At that time, the weight of town growth moved from the frontiers toward the center. Southern Italian commerce played second fiddle to that of North Italy by the end of the eleventh century. Towns in Flanders and Picardy moved ahead of the seaports of the North and Baltic seas.

By the twelfth century, the central axis of European commerce had been established. It ran from Flanders through the Champagne and Rhineland, down the Rhone valley to Liguria and Lombardy. Thence the Pisans, Genoese, and Venetians sailed to the eastern Mediterranean. By the end of the thirteenth century, expanding western commerce had filled all France and most of Spain with towns and trade routes. A direct sea route from the Mediterranean to Flanders was created. The northern and eastern German plains bloomed during the fourteenth century, and new towns multiplied east of the Elbe river. At the same time, Baltic and North sea commerce reached its apogee under the direction of the German Hanse, or league of northern towns.

As commerce and industry multiplied, the towns themselves grew larger. At their peak in the early fourteenth century, however, the largest western cities rarely boasted a population of 100,000. Milan and Venice were among the few towns that surpassed this number. (*See Document No. 4.*) By far the greatest northern town, Paris had about 80,000 souls. Naturally enough, urbanism developed more in some than in other areas. After Lombardy, the second greatest urban area was Flanders. Her great towns averaged from twenty to forty thousand souls. Languedoc may be cited as a region of modest town: Toulouse probably attained 25,000, Beziers 14,000, Carcassonne 10,000. A relatively backward area, England, had only one great town: London, with about 40,000 inhabitants. (*See Document No. 5.*)

As is evident, parts of Europe were more developed than others. Flanders and north Italy were predominantly urban. This statement, however, must be put in context. During the middle ages, indeed, until the industrial revolution, Europe was essentially agrarian. But, with this in mind, it is certain that the economic relationship of areas of strong town life to those of weak explains a great deal of the medieval epoch. The Plantagenet empire sometimes seems to be almost an appendage to the great cloth manufacturing towns of Flanders. Bordeaux and Poitou supplied wine and grain and England exported wool to this urban market. The importance of this commerce for the relations of the kings of France and of England is obvious. French control over Flanders would have been decisive not only for England's trade. It would also have weakened the English king's independence from his barons. In 1297, the barons claimed that the royal tax on exported wool equaled a fifth part of the value of the whole land of England.

An even more impressive example of the relationship of heavily urban areas to their sources of supply is seen in Italy. It was estimated in the late thirteenth century that Florence could feed itself from its own territory for only five months of the year. In 1261, 2,200 tons of Sicilian grain entered the port of Genoa alone. In the early fourteenth century, Sicily exported 86,000 quarters of grain to northern Italy in one year. Apulia and Calabria exported meat and hides for Lombard towns. Besides, southern Italy lay athwart the routes of communication to the Near East. These mutual dependencies led to conflict, a conflict that was part of the great struggle between popes and emperors. In the late twelfth and early thirteenth centuries, the north triumphed over the south, and Pisans and Genoese occupied Sicily's seaports. The second stage of this struggle began with a southern counter-attack but ended in a northern victory with the political disintegration of the south by 1285. (*See Document No. 8.*)

To conclude our general observations on the rise of towns, the most consequential achievement of the medieval period was the development of northern Europe. This marked a great step in the migration of civilization and its urban form from the Mediterranean. Before this time, urbanism had initially been associated with large

rivers, as in the "hydraulic" societies of Egypt and Meso-
potamia. Classic Greece and Rome extended this civilization along the coasts and savannahs of the *Mare
Nostrum*. The middle ages spread it to the inland areas
of a continent. The development of a continental civilization based upon the extensive northern plain was the
great advantage that enabled Europe to conquer the
world in modern times.

But we may not overestimate the medieval achievement. The shift to the north was not yet quite so great as
it seems at first glance. The weightiest center of medieval
town life was Lombardy, along the Po river and its con-
fluents. Rome had already settled the Lombard upland
plains; medieval man only extended the area under cultivation. Of the vast northern plain, only the region from
Flanders to Paris or Orléans was yet capable of supporting a first class concentration of towns. This was certainly
an enormously significant region. It invented the style
called Gothic and was the home of a French culture that
was the peer of the ecclesiastic's Latinity. The French
language was spoken from Ireland to the Near East in the
thirteenth century. Nevertheless, most of the northern
plain was only lightly settled. Its towns were small. It was
only during modern times that it realized its full poten-
tial.

Commerce. As the town grew, so did its commerce. In the ninth and tenth centuries, it was primitive
and restricted. The autarkic tradition of decentralized
society had cut commerce to the minimum. No matter
how self-sufficient the centers of this early time were,
however, records of merchant voyages and peasant transport services attest that trade went on. Metalware and
salt were at all times imported by most western communities. More, autarky itself embodies a basic contradiction. A monastery such as St. Trond sought to live of its
own on domains spread from Trier in the Rhineland to
Nimwegen in Holland. But this design necessitated an
exchange of goods: Trier supplied wine, Nimwegen grain.
Furthermore, autarky does not mean dislike of profit.
Tenth century Lombard monasteries regularly sold their
surplus to the budding centers of Pavia and Venice.

Besides, there was always some trade in luxuries and
cultural goods. Byzantine cloth, Arabic weapons, and

eastern spices were fairly regularly imported. So were ideas and learning. Given a certain level of civilization, these commodities were as important as salt and grain. We have already spoken about the Byzantine and Islamic educational function. A first-class Cluniac monastery had to have a Greek book or two. Much of the social and hospital work performed by monasteries in this early age was learned in Byzantium. However poorly, education had to be paid for, and this importation demanded export in return.

Western exports in this early period are not well known, and it may be presumed that the balance of trade was always unfavorable. As we have already seen, slaves were sold to Islam to get gold to buy in Byzantium. Doubtless, there were other commodities, but the west boasted little industry and not much more surplus food. It is evident, then, that Europe did not devote much effort to commerce. This is shown by the fact that the principal intermediaries between Islam and the west were the Jews. Slave runners, shipowners, great travelers, they were more eastern than western in mores, being, for example, polygamous. As merchants, they were protected and exploited by princely privilege. Jews, however, enjoyed no monopoly. There were Baltic German merchants. Venice sold slaves as did the Jews, and the products it brought back from Byzantium were sold through Pavia to the west.

What is significant about early long-range commerce is the contrast it offers to the intensely local trade in salt, metals, and victuals. Up to the eleventh century, there was little intermediate commerce to bridge the gap. From that time on, however, all commerce grew, but the medium range grew most of all. English wool, Bordeaux wine, Sicilian grain are examples. The trade pattern with the Byzantine and Moslem Mediterranean changed too. Western metalware and building techniques penetrated there. Flemish cloth reached these markets by the end of the twelfth century. Commerce of every kind expanded enormously, and its significance is clearly illustrated by an entry in the account book of a Stockholm merchant. In 1328, the good Esterling sold a Swedish noble family 1½ pounds of saffron derived from Spain or Italy, 12 pounds of kummel and 90 of almonds from the Mediterranean, 4¾ pounds of Indian ginger, a half pound of

grains of paradise from west Africa, 1 pound of Singha-
lese cinnamon, 6 pounds of pepper from the Malabar
coast, 3 pounds of anis from southern Germany and 3 of
galangal from south Asia, 105 pounds of rice and 4 of
sugar from Spain, and three barrels of wine, one Rhine
and two French.

Europe's trade balance with the east remained deficient.
It paid for purchases not so much by export as by domination. Its marine monopolized all but purely local transportation in the Mediterranean and Black seas. Its merchants penetrated through the Near East to China and
the Indian Ocean. Based on Ormuz, the Genoese proposed
in 1300 to station a squadron off Aden to interrupt Egyp-
tian traffic. European military power wrung subsidies of
precious metals from Islamic states. Traders and mis-
sionaries penetrated the gold-producing Senegal and Sudan. Writing in the late thirteenth century, Peter Dubois
urged Europe to revive the crusade, conquer the Near
East definitively, and thereby assure a cheap supply of
spices. Europe's triumph was evidenced by the minting
of gold, particularly the Florentine florin of 1252 and
the Venetian ducat of 1284. These were the first gold
coins of any importance for trade minted in the west since
the seventh century. Byzantine and Islamic coins disappeared: Latin commerce had come of age.

Transportation. Trade involves transportation. It
may be stated as a general—indeed, as an obvious—rule
that the most inexpensive way to transport goods in bulk
was by sea. This was one reason why the Mediterranean
played so central a role in both antiquity and the middle
ages. Perhaps, then, the most significant medieval maritime achievements were to make the Baltic and North
seas into another, if lesser, *Mare Nostrum,* and to link
the two areas together by a direct route from Italy to
Flanders around 1300. On the other hand, medieval ships
themselves were not very impressive. In the thirteenth
century, a large Venetian vessel was 110 feet long, and a
moderate-sized Genoese ship carried over 175 crewmen
and passengers. These sizes do not compare with that of
the grain ships that ran from Ostia to Alexandria in ancient times. But size is not the only criterion. In the later
middle ages, the interplay of the northern and Mediterranean maritime areas produced inventions that made the

exploitation of the Atlantic possible. The rudder, the articulation of sails, and the development of navigation and mapmaking were all medieval innovations.

Perhaps the most important medieval advance was the development of transportation within a continental area, by river and road. Ancient society had, of course, made use of rivers: the Tigris-Euphrates and the Nile are well known. The coastal civilization of the Romans, however, was less river-oriented. It made use of rivers already opened by nature: the Rhone, Rhine, and Danube, for instance. But the Romans left the Po and Garonne marshy and choked by forests. In antiquity, also, most German rivers were little more than meandering swamps. All this was changed during the middle ages. Valleys were reduced to cultivation and river channels were established. Naturally, some rivers were of only limited use: the swift flowing Rhone was uneconomical for long-distance upstream traffic. Medieval man also lacked the means to create a network of canals for shipping such as enlivened Europe in the seventeenth and eighteenth centuries. Canals were dug, but largely for drainage or irrigation.

At first sight, medieval roads seem incomparably inferior to Roman. Roman roads were paved, whereas, except in towns, medieval ones were not. On the other hand, Roman roads were designed largely for travelers on foot. Medieval roads were suitable for horses and pack animals, whose hoofs were hurt by hard surfaces. In fact, the generalization of the use of the horse in the medieval period required that roads not be paved—as indeed they were not in Europe until the automotive age. Moreover, the settlement of continental Europe required a far larger route network than the Romans had possessed. As commerce expanded, town statutes and seignorial legislation everywhere encouraged road building and maintenance. (*See Documents Nos. 9C, 38A, 46F.*) Admitting the advantages of horse and pack animal transportation, the road system it created posed difficulties: transport and commerce were pretty much restricted to summer and autumn.

The periodicity of commercial activity reminds us of another aspect of medieval trade: the fair. The universality of the fair throughout the west illustrates the episodic character of long- and medium-range trade. We do not mean that business ceased between fairs. Industry and local trade continued. Moreover, large centers, such as Marseille and Genoa, were active the year around despite seasonal fluctuations. Essentially, the fair reflected limitations imposed by technology and the seasons.

Fair types were varied. No absolute distinction can be drawn between a village market and a town fair. Except that one was local and the other inter-regional, their essential functions were the same. That the institution of the fair could become highly specialized, however, is shown by the twelfth and thirteenth century Champagne fairs. Four Champagne towns developed a rotating system of six fairs that lasted most of the year. They provided warehouses, expeditious justice, and other conveniences for merchants. Champagne developed this specialty because it lay on the main axis of western trade, from Flanders to Lombardy, and because its location gave easy access to the valley roads and waterways of the Rhone, Rhine, Meuse, Seine and Loire. For a time, the Champagne fairs served as a clearing house for European business.

To expedite commerce, merchants and their towns formed associations. The merchant gilds of north Europe are famous and shall be discussed. Town leagues were also built. (*See Documents Nos. 43, 44.*) Cloth manufacturing Flanders formed two Hanses, or gilds: one, of twenty-two towns, to buy wool in England, the other, of seventeen, to regulate marketing at the Champagne fairs. Twenty-two towns and gilds met at Orléans to maintain navigation along the Loire river in the thirteenth century. The same century saw the alliance of Hamburg and Lübeck, starting the famous Hanse of Baltic and North sea towns that controlled northern trade into the fifteenth century. Trade very often implies dominance. Italian merchants were not satisfied to trade in Byzantium. They lived there in their own fortified quarter protected by extraterritorial rights. The later Hanseatic Steelyards sometimes equaled the Italian *fondaco*. At Bergen, the Esterling settlement was connected to the native town by the Bridge of Lice. (*See Documents Nos. 56, 60.*)

Industry and Investment. Industry kept commerce moving. Although production was sometimes impressive, individual enterprise was small scale. That there were big industrialists is shown by the example of John Boine Broke of thirteenth century Douai. But, while some individuals had their fingers in many pies, the pies themselves were rather small. Cloth, for example, was produced in small workshops, and the industry organized on the domestic system. (*See Documents Nos. 41, 50.*) Other than foodstuffs, cloth was Europe's most important export commodity. Flemish and Italian woolens sold to rich and poor alike. Two examples will suffice to show that medieval industry was varied and well developed:

In 1292, Paris had 130 regulated professions: 18 dealt in alimentation and consumption goods such as firewood, 5 in building and monumental arts, 22 in metallurgy, 22 in textiles and leather, 36 in clothing and personal furnishings, 10 in house furniture, 3 in medicine and sanitation, and 15 in divers specialties, including banking, brokerage, and bookmaking.

In the 1340s, the Champagne town of Provins had a population of from 8 to 10,000 in town and in 8 villages outside. In a plebiscite, 1,741 votes were cast by townsmen and 960 by villagers. 900 voters were in the textile industry, 450 in other technical professions, and 500 worked in the vines and fields. All told, 100 different trades were mentioned. 350 voters were women, presumably widowed heads of households and workshops.

The import of medieval industry must not be exaggerated. It is true that, by the thirteenth century, Latin metal and building techniques surpassed those of the Near East. But the medieval period did not mark a great advance over antiquity. In fact, it may be argued that there was no basic technological change since the introduction of settled agriculture, domesticated animals, metal work, and town life in the late neolithic age until yesterday's industrial revolution. Both antiquity and the middle ages are alike in being times when already known techniques were transplanted to new areas.

A further urban business was investment in land and building. Construction was an early source of wealth, and many large fortunes were made in it and in real estate. This partly explains why princes and nobles were often as interested in encouraging town growth as the burghers themselves. Also, the rich burgher or urban knight not

only owned rents and housing in town, he usually acquired and operated dairies, stock farms, or other exploitations in the environs. Contracts by which town dwellers
capitalized rural enterprise are known from the eleventh
century, particularly concerning the raising of animals
for wool, hides, or meat.

Investment calls to mind ways by which enterprises
gained capital and were organized. The most characteristic twelfth and thirteenth century method was to form
societates not unlike modern partnerships. The partners
often shared investment and labor equally. Frequently,
however, one partner or a group invested capital, tools,
or facilities in others' labor. Contractual forms were varied as were their names, and derived from a variety of
legal traditions. The revived Roman law of twelfth century Bologna was particularly noteworthy because it sys-
tematized local practices. Basic aspects of the western
business society, however, seem related to the agrarian
world in which it was born. Max Weber has pointed out
how similar business partnerships were to the family partnerships—*frèrêché,* in French—so common in rural society. The *commenda* also seems closely filiated to service
contracts known to feudal and domanial practice.

By the device of shares, partnerships were able to
mobilize considerable capital for specific enterprises. The
most spectacular examples of this are to be found in shipping. One Genoese adventure of the thirteenth century
was subdivided into seventy shares. The partnership had
other advantages. Flexible and simple, it was suited to the
business of small communities. On the other hand, most
partnerships were small-scale affairs. Besides, all partners
bore full responsibility. Within the terms of the contract,
each was guarantor for the debts of the whole. Such societies lacked perpetuity, also, being created for a specific
voyage, for example, or a stated length of time. Everything depended upon the personal relationships of the
partners. In short, the medieval business society seems
casual and petty, lacking continuity and predictability.
(*See Documents Nos. 57, 58, 60.*)

The real sense of continuity was given business by the
family. Family enterprise made the fortunes of the Bardi,
Peruzzi, Frescobaldi, and the other merchants and bankers of Florence and Siena in the thirteenth and early

fourteenth centuries. That business organization along
family lines has weaknesses is evident. It limits the accumulation of capital. When an investor put money "in
deposit," as they said then, he gambled on the reputation
of the individual or family. The same is true, of course,
of a modern corporation, but the risk is more widely
shared. The guarantees afforded a modern investor are
paralleled in this early time only by investment in the
state, as at Genoa from the latter twelfth century. (*See
Document No. 54.*) But family enterprise was characteristic of the age; perhaps an age of expansion does not
exact elaborate guarantees.

The western economy matured by the early fourteenth
century. The complexity of its business agencies may be
seen in banking. From pawnshops to the great mercantile
and investment houses of the Bardi and Peruzzi, a wide
range of institutions created credit. Commercial banks
sometimes overdid it and crashed. The assets of one late
fourteenth century Barcelona bank were only 16 per cent
specie, those of a Bruges bank in 1370, 29.3 per cent
specie. Although rates of interest were high, profit was
not extortionate. From 1308 to 1324, the Peruzzi's annual gain averaged from 14 per cent to 20 per cent before
expenses.

A variety of agencies and special social groups helped
the western businessman. Into the early fourteenth century, their common characteristic was universality. One
of these was the church, particularly its crusading orders,
the Hospitallers and Templars. The Templars' prime economic function was safekeeping and transporting specie,
largely from Europe to the Near East. The Templars
therefore became treasurers for Europe's kings. The Hospitallers invested in land and erected hospitals throughout
Europe. Both orders offered facilities analogous to modern safe deposit vaults.

The Jews were another Europe-wide group. Their status
had changed considerably by the twelfth century, commercial presidency having been stripped from them by
the rise of Christian merchants. They became dealers in
money, permitted a higher rate of interest by civil law
than their Christian competitors. In spite of sporadic
persecutions in the late eleventh and early twelfth centuries and constant popular hostility, Jewish communities

generally flourished until the late thirteenth century and assimilated greatly in mores, though rarely in religion, to the culture around them. (*See Documents Nos. 38B, 44.*)

Business leadership fell to northern Italians, Lombards or Tuscans, during the late twelfth and the thirteenth centuries. They enjoyed advantages that gave them superiority in trade and credit techniques. Northern Italy equaled Flanders in industry, but, because it lay on the main axis of commerce from north Europe to the eastern Mediterranean, it far surpassed Flanders in commerce. Moreover, the close alliance between the Lombards and the papacy made them partners of the papal king of kings. As his agents and bankers, they had entrée everywhere. For a while, Europe almost became tributary to Lombard enterprise. Italian mercantile and banking firms stationed factors from England to Cyprus.

Town Planning. Urban expansion was represented in other ways than building, industry, and commerce. Townsmen were interested in improving their community's facilities, for example, with public baths or bridges. (*See Document No. 38A.*) Moreover, there was an important religious element in these activities. During a town's early days, for example, the clergy frequently financed bridge construction. Bridge tolls were often collected not only for maintenance but also for hospitals. Town fathers endeavored to preserve the proprieties. Laws on social convention abound and every town law had provisions prohibiting the casual disposition of garbage and regulating open sewers. (*See Document No. 38C.*)

More significant is the appearance of town planning. Early medieval centers, notably the northern bourgs, were dominated by defense needs. They, therefore, tended to be nuclear or radial in street plan, and their walls somewhat circular. They were adapted to the terrain, in order to utilize it for defense. Besides, old Roman cities had been lived in for generations and had long lost their initial regularity and straightness. Well into the eleventh century, the western town was sort of higgledy-piggledy. The new urbanism of the twelfth century, however, began to use planning.

By no means the only form, the simple rectangular grid was the most usual plan. New sections of older towns, such as Carcassonne and Hildesheim, were laid out in this style. But it was only in wholly new settlements that the form could attain full stature. Aigues Mortes, St. Louis' crusading port, was built all of a piece and laid out in a grid. Perhaps the greatest successes of town planning were the small new towns or villages—*villeneuves* or *bastides,* as they were called in France—the plan of whose fields and urban nuclei were all dominated by this simple rational pattern. Here is evidence that ideas born in the towns invaded and structured the countryside.

The use of the term "rational" should not mislead. There is something wonderfully irrational about the application to nature of man's reason. Rivers do not flow around right angles, nor do plateaus form perfect squares. More than anything else, perhaps, the imposition of a mathematically satisfying scheme upon nature's irregularity illustrates man's self-assurance during the twelfth and thirteenth centuries.

— 4 —

TOWN, COUNTRY, AND PRINCE: THE SEARCH FOR LIBERTY

Until the twelfth century, at least, a sharp distinction between town and country is not discernible. First, the difference in size of town and village was not yet great. Second, functional specialization had not yet matured. Admittedly, there was no rural parallel to the long-range merchant. But many in the villages sought to profit from functions other than administration and farming. Millers, smiths, and quasi-servile administrative personnel—ministers, as they were called—were almost infamous for lending money and serving as brokers and local traders. Like towns, moreover, the village or rather villages gathered into seignories or larger castellanies in the eleventh and twelfth centuries had a real, if not irrefragible, awareness of common and local interest. As castellanies grew, tolls and tariffs proliferated. Sometimes an indirect means of encouraging trade, many such tolls financed the creation of transport facilities. But there was another motive that reflected the decentralization of Europe's economy. Collected on almost everything, these taxes impeded trade and protected village and small town commerce and industry.

Localism is the necessary consequence of decentralization and was almost as characteristic of the town as of the village. The town's economic design was the same as its politics: freedom from all. While there were urban leagues for common purposes, economic and even political relationships between towns were regulated by the laws of marque and reprisal. A merchant could be seized by the authorities of neighboring towns as gage for payment of debts by his home community or for restitution of damage inflicted by one of his concitizens. To the later jurists of Europe's national era, this localist law of marque and reprisal seemed barbaric and unsystematic. But it was the natural expression of a localized economy and sense of sovereignty.

Localism, then, was of fundamental importance to western urbanism. We wonder why the incomparably rich plains of the north did not produce towns equal in size to ancient Rome, medieval Byzantium, or even those of the Andean Indians. These same plains fed the great towns of early modern Europe and witnessed the birth of the industrial revolution. We may argue that Europe's towns were inland, and that, until the railroad, no center other than a port could grow to great size. But the Lowlands and North France lay on a coast renowned for harbors and watered by one of the greatest concentration of navigable rivers found anywhere in the world. The answer seems to be neither technological nor economic. The separatism that destroyed Rome seems to have engendered a jealous localism and sense of identity that prevented the rise of the giant city in the medieval age.

The lack of megalopolitan centers, however, does not imply that towns did not have an advantage over the countryside in the eleventh and twelfth century expansion. Everything grew, but the towns, the larger agglomerations, grew fastest. Communication centers, they directed and guided the expansion of the regions around them. Moreover, urban growth was aided by the mutual interest of town and country. Harmony was expressed not only in economics but also in politics. (*See Document No. 44.*) The rural lords and castellans sought freedom from the greater princes. So did the townsmen. Seignorial privileges and town liberties had the same source: they devolved from the courts of princes and kings.

Common interest, however, did not obliterate the hostility between town and country. This enmity was only overtly expressed in the matured society of the thirteenth century, but premonitory signs were not lacking in earlier ages. Once relatively liberated from its own lord, the town was free to attack those of the villages or smaller towns outside of its walls. It was often aided in this task by conflicts within the countryside. An instance of this was the struggle within the rural aristocracy, continuing the trend of decentralizing or devolving power. In the Burgundies, for example, the large castellany reached its peak during the twelfth century. Smaller village groupings replaced it, the typical seignory of the thirteenth century. While the might of the town increased, then, the countryside suffered further subdivision.

As consequent in weakening rural resistance was the villagers' desire to reduce the services they owed their lords. Like townsmen, they sought freedom from tax, service, and social controls such as those on marriage and inheritance. Known in France as *corvée, formariage,* and *mortmain,* these obligations summed up what the villein owed his *villa* or village. They were the medieval version of the duties owed by all men to the state in which they live. Oppressed or in search of greater opportunities, the villager could move to town. There, he was protected by the town peace, guarding its citizens against pursuit and seizure. Once resident beyond immediate recall and having performed his civic duties, the countryman became a citizen. "Town air makes free," to use a famous phrase— free, that is, to be a citizen of urban *villae* and not of the *villae* and *castella* of the countryside. (*See Documents Nos. 23, 25.*)

Another way the village was weakened was by encouraging the peasants to emancipate themselves from their lords, thereby attenuating the jurisdictional unity of the little rural state or seignory. That this was done primarily for the townsmen themselves is amply evidenced. Highhanded abolition of local tolls, penetration of villages by town money lenders, judicial advantages given townsmen in urban courts, and retention in bondage of countryfolk who owed services to burghers illustrate the self-interest that veils itself in the love of others' liberty. But these deleterious aspects of the relation of villein to burgher were but a small part of twelfth century experience. Men of that age could reasonably hope that the restoration of man to his "natural liberty" was both virtuous and profitable.

The North and the Mediterranean. The relationship of town to countryside and, therefore, the form of urbanism itself varied widely in Europe. But there were also basic similarities. In the early ages, for example, the town served as a communication and administrative center for its rural ambiance. Episcopal leadership was general in most towns, save those of the furthest peripheries, as England and Scandinavia. The system of regulated and functional orders giving service to the community was inherited from late Rome and continued to lend order to social life. Lastly, while electoral institutions existed, the principal form of state was monarchy or princely government. Whether the prince was king, bishop, or simple lord, his tradition came from Constantine and Charlemagne.

But the similarities can almost be taken for granted. What interests us here are distinctions. Edith Ennen has recently emphasized the difference between the southern urban form derived from Rome and the new town life of the north. Mediterranean town society was more mature than that which first emerged in the north during the medieval period. In general, also, Mediterranean towns had not suffered so severely during the dark ages of invasion, and they were directly in touch with really vibrant urbanism, such as Byzantium. For these reasons, the particularly well protected areas of Lombardy and Tuscany preserved a large portion of antiquity's urban tradition. When the Italian towns began to revive, they were able, therefore, first to educate the urbanism of adjacent regions, such as Provence, and then slowly the rest of Europe.

The eleventh century Italian town served as the capital of its province. The word *civitas,* or city, meant not only the town but also the region about it, the county or diocese. The rise of episcopal presidency, however, signals the emergence of independent jurisdictional centers in the countryside. Seeking to weaken the separatist power of its secular functionaries, the counts, the empire strengthened the Lombard bishops as early as 867. While retaining some hold in town, therefore, the counts increasingly rested their real strength on their possessions in the countryside. Elsewhere in Italy and southern France, secular princes retained town direction. But when they they did, their vicars and viscounts in smaller towns and villages destroyed the old uniform jurisdiction of the city.

In many ways, the frontier urbanism of north Europe moved in the same direction. It began with the same tradition of administrative unity. The fortified bourgs built in Flanders in the tenth and eleventh centuries were intended to be government centers. But the tradition was weaker up north. Even the old Roman cities along the Rhine and Meuse and in northern France had lost more rural jurisdiction than the Italian by the eleventh century. In Italy, the word *suburb* still meant the general region around the town; in France and the Lowlands, it referred only to the immediate environs. In short, when towns began again to rise, the difference between north and south was one of degree. Southern urbanism was stronger than northern.

When expanding, the direction the two urbanisms took was similar. Northern towns tried to extend their power over the countryside, and were sometimes capable of it. The old city of Metz, for example, ruled no less than 168 villages. Even little Provins in the Champagne had a *banlieue* comprising 8 villages. And these instances were typical. But Metz could not compare with huge Milan that, by the fourteenth century, extended its sway over whole provinces, towns and villages alike. Because theirs was a frontier and ofttimes new urbanism, northerners did not equal the achievements of the Italian or even the southern French republics. In the north, burgher law often worriedly prohibited rural knights and magnates from living in town. In Italy, town law frequently obliged them to live there. (*See Documents Nos. 6, 30, 42.*)

Another significant contrast between north and south is to be seen in the social groups within the community. In Italy, artisans, merchants, and knights or state officers

were domiciled within the same walls. True, these groups
were differentiated by law according to function and
wealth. But the late Roman tradition of function and
service to the community, although simplified, brought
them all together. Officialdom ran the whole gamut from
important captains or castellans through simple knights
or knight-ministers down to ministerial minters and toll
collectors. These lesser grades were hardly distinguishable
from *negociatores,* merchants or businessmen. From castellan to merchant, all owed service. The difference was
simply one of function. The higher grades owed administrative and military service while the lower largely owed
money and goods. As a result, the equivalence of the
knight with the burgher who lived nobly was early developed in the southern town. (*See Documents Nos. 6, 33.*)

The Northern Merchant.   Some tenth century northern towns, particularly the cities of Roman foundation,
were much like their Italian counterparts. Most, however,
were either too new or too small to produce the inter-
mediary social grades that tied the military aristocracy to
the merchants so successfully in Italy. Moreover, being
on a frontier, military considerations played a great part
in building the nuclei of later northern towns, the *castra*
or fortified bourgs. Originally—and continuously in the
south—meaning an unfortified market place, the Roman
word *bourg* came to mean a fortified center in the north.
Eleventh century Flemish bourgs, for example, were gar-
rison and administrative posts. True, other social groups
resided there: occasional merchants and artisans. But they
were few, and, where there were more, as in the old cities
of Roman foundation, they were often of the foreign caste
of Jewish merchants.

There were merchants other than Jews, however, in
northern Europe. But they rarely lived in the bourg or
even in the city. They usually settled outside the walls in
an emporium, often called a port, *vicus,* or *Wik.* The *Wik*
merchant, moreover, was unlike the southern *negociator.*
Like Homer's traders, he was a wanderer, not a merchant
domiciled in a town. His settlement was an emporium
where he came to trade, not to live. For this reason the
privileges of free movement and exemption from service
were usually granted by northern monarchs to merchants
but not to towns in the tenth century. A caste outside of

settled society, merchants were treated by legislators in almost the same way as were Jews. "Jews and other merchants," went the traditional phrase. It was only in the eleventh century that merchants settled down and became citizens of a community. Then merchant law and privilege became the muniment of a town or part of a town. (*See Document No. 21.*)

For these reasons, the *Wik* was always an area of special jurisdiction. The northern town was two towns: a merchant settlement hard up against a fortified administrative center. As peace returned in the tenth and eleventh centuries, the bourg and the expanding *Wik* occasionally fused together. By the twelfth century, many German towns, for example, had councils composed of burghers and of knights or ministers. On the whole, however, this was not characteristic. Generations of special law reinforced the merchant's peculiarity. This distinction between northern and southern urbanism is shown in the history of the words citizen (*civis*) and burgher (*burgensis*).

The word citizen described the inhabitant of the Mediterranean town, whether knight or commoner. Burgher was also used but primarily referred to one who inhabited a bourg. It will be recalled that the Mediterranean bourg was generally a market settlement outside the city walls. This fact early gave the word burgher a secondary and social meaning, implying that a burgher was usually in trade, hence a plebeian. In the north, citizen also meant an inhabitant of an old city. But it retreated before the word burgher, newly introduced to the north in the latter eleventh century from the Mediterranean. Bourg in the north customarily meant a fortified center, having little to do with merchants. The inhabitants of the *Wik* had usually been called portmen or simply merchants. The foreign style burgher reflected their new awareness that they were townsmen. The adoption of this term changed its meaning. Because northern merchants did not live in a bourg, the geographical sense that was so strong in the Mediterranean disappeared. All that was left was social distinction: the northern townsman or burgher could not be a knight.

The political evolution of the northern town, furthermore, tells a similar story. It usually evolved in two directions. When, as in maritime Flanders, the bourg was swallowed by the growing *Wik,* its jurisdiction split in two: a town jurisdiction as against a rural one. The bourg's inhabitants either became burghers or migrated to the countryside. When, as at Liège, the bourg remained strong, it lost jurisdiction over the merchant settlement only, retaining its own government and that of the countryside. Whatever the course, the distinction between town and country and between knight and burgher was formalized in a way unknown to the Mediterranean.

By itself, the frontier simplicity of northern urbanism does not adequately explain this distinction of town types. There are other sides of this problem that bear investigation. The north is often described as more "feudal" than the south. If this term implies more of a split between town and country, it is true. But if we mean by it that royal or princely authority was less vigorous in the north than in the south, we are in error. Until the end of the eleventh century, the centers of all important states were in the north. State power devolved and decentralized everywhere, but the memory of Charlemagne, relatively primitive social structure, and frontier defense needs retained greater state power in the north than in the south. The German empire, the duchies and counties of northern France possessed centralized administrations unparalleled in the south save in the marches of Spain. From Languedoc through most of Italy, effective state power was in rapid decline. These regions invented the Peace of God, that ecclesiastical supplement for weakening secular police, and, from time to time, invited northern princes to come and restore social quiet. (*See Document No. 6.*)

This difference in state power reinforced the distinction between the urban aristocracies of north and south. In the late eleventh century, northern town knights and officers were still largely ministerial, that is to say, lacking hereditary rights and formal delimitation of duties. In Lombardy or Provence, the picture was different. The distant German emperor slowed the loss of his power by granting liberty or hereditary rights to ever lesser elements of the governmental hierarchy. Imperial policy had fostered the bishop and captain or castellan against the separatist dukes and counts. By the mid-eleventh century, ancient friends had become enemies. The emperors then privileged the lesser knights. The celebrated grant of 1037, for example, guaranteed the Milanese little vassals hereditary right to office and emolument, trial by peers, and other liberties of the higher orders.

By the late eleventh century attack on princely power, the Lombard and Provencal knights had already gained all they could hope to from the prince. They were aware of their order's value, and were envied and emulated by the rest of the citizenry. They served as leaders of community endeavour. In the north, while this was sometimes the case, the ministerial knighthood was more straightly bound to its prince. When the town rebelled, the ministers either lost the town, gaining knightly status in defence of their prince, or surrendered a not yet wholly honorable status to join the burghers. As a result, the peculiar freedoms that tradition associated with the wandering merchants of the *Wik* came to symbolize the northern town's search for freedom.

Town Freedom. Whatever the form, towns sought freedom everywhere. The movement began in Italy, then reached the more developed sections of northern Europe: Flanders, the Meuse, and the Rhineland. Thence it spread everywhere. The first great urban victories were won at the turn of the eleventh and twelfth centuries. As we have seen, what was true of the town was true of the countryside. Everywhere, princely power suffered attack and devolved or decentralized another stage. There is, however, a distinction between the way in which this power devolved upon towns and rural areas. Exceptions aside, political power or seignory (*potestas*) was exercised in the villages by dynasties. The basic rural political structure was therefore princely. The existence in the town of a number of families of equal might weakened the dynastic possibility. The typical form, therefore, was the exercise of power by a *universitas* or association, in short, a collective seignory. Municipal political form was consequently republican. (*See Document No. 15.*)

The town desired "to hold" of God and to hold of no other. To be ruled by God alone is to be free to do what one wants. Marseille's In-God-We-Trust, for example, paralleled the princely ambition to rule *gratia Dei* or the seignor's to hold "of the Sun." (*See Document No. 43.*) That so high an aim could rarely be achieved is obvious.

Most towns had to be content with the development of a customary law that guaranteed their inhabitants personal liberty and limited their princes' rights in fiscal, judicial, and other matters. (*See Documents Nos. 22, 26, 28, 32.*) Even the strongest Lombard towns never wholly dispensed with the emperor's lordship, however theoretical it became. But that they sought and attained sovereignty is shown by the titles of their elected magistrates. The first was that of consul. (*See Document No. 6.*) The Roman origin of this title and its implications are obvious. Moreover, consul was a customary, if somewhat rhetorical title, applied to secular princes in the eleventh century. Much employed in the west to mean seignory, the second term was *potestas.* Many Italian towns won so great a measure of freedom from their nominal princes that a new and real head of state was necessary, particularly for foreign affairs and war. During the latter twelfth century, therefore, the elected office of the *potestas,* or supreme magistrate, appeared in Italy. (*See Document No. 14.*)

Northern achievements in the struggle with princes were not so prepossessing. The consulate, tocsin of town liberty, spread from Italy. Its progress was rapid around the Mediterranean, in southern France and elsewhere. North of the Alps, however, it entered late and moved slowly, becoming frequent in German towns, for example, only by the thirteenth century. In general, less republican titles were utilized. But it is unwise to underline this distinction too heavily: new urban government forms were basically similar in both north and south.

The Italian consulate derived from the old princely court or council. This is shown by the fact that the consuls usually numbered from four to twelve, or a multiple thereof: the six assessors, or *scabini,* the four judges who read the law, and the two advocates who protected the church. Oft changed by local needs, this constitution had its origin in the legislation of Charlemagne and his successors. While asserting the princely investment right, this antique law encouraged election. The electoral tradition reminds us that the prince had always called on community leaders to participate in his court or council. Indeed, he often invested those whom the community chose. Upon the formalization of town associations in the late eleventh century and after, the princely court and council either became a body of magistrates elected by the community and titled consuls or fell under the dominance of the town's consuls. In general terms, then, what happened in the period of the developing consulate was that the once princely officialdom became that of the town *universitas*. (*See Document No. 9A and B.*)

Much the same evolution often took place in the north. The mayors are weakly analogous to the *potestates* of Italy. In Flemish towns, the *scabini*, or assessors, became the elected representatives of the urban association. There are, however, several significant departures from this pattern. One is the institution of the *jurati*. While they sometimes ruled a whole town, these sworn representatives of an urban association initially and usually represented only a portion, that part which had its origin in the merchant community or *Wik*. When we see at Liège the old *scabini* of the bourg still meeting together while the rest of the town was governed by *jurati*, we are reminded of the typical northern pattern: the split between knights and merchants and the division between town and countryside. Unlike its Italian counterpart, therefore, the northern *universitas* was rarely strong enough to capture the whole of the old administration.

Social conflict between town groups or between town and country were means by which a prince retained his power. His attempt was not simply a self-interested design to play one group against another. Social arbitration is a reason for princely government. The rise to predominance of any one group or interest necessarily threatened the prince, and, in this age of growing towns, caused him to combat urban liberty. In spite of efforts to hold the line, however, princely might retreated everywhere. (*See Document No. 31.*) While part of this process was the result of the town's desire for liberty and the general devolution of princely power in every sphere, part was stimulated by the role of the church in the eleventh and twelfth centuries.

The Church and Urbanism. A vast and myriad order, the clergy played many roles in this crucial period. Where bishops were princely, as they often were, they fought as princes. (*See Document No. 11.*) But there was another side to the church, more significant than the exercise of princely prerogative. Even the prince-bishops of the Meuse-Rhine area and of Lombardy were not real princes before the twelfth century. They were simply imperial officers. When they gained their freedom from the empire, that act obliged townsmen to seek, and the emperor to grant, town liberties. Even inadvertently, then, the desire of the clergy for freedom fostered that of townsmen. Still clearer is the case of a prelate who enjoyed no secular office and who was subjected to princely caesaro-papism. Instanced in Tuscany, Provence, and Languedoc, the loss of the prince was the gain of both town and bishop. A common and advertent interest bound them together. The bishop emerged as the moderator of social strife, sometimes even as president of the town association.

In a more general sense, we recall that the church was traditionally the lesser partner and subject of the state. During the eleventh and twelfth centuries, this relationship was reversed. Fired by the monks and mobilized by the papacy, the ecclesiastical order sought and obtained liberty. In seeking freedom for itself, the church necessarily implemented the achievement of the same of all men. Churchmen stood to gain from the decentralization and devolution of secular powers. It is no accident that seignorial and urban liberties reached their maximum effectual development at the same moment that the popes reached the apogee of their power.

We must be moderate. What has been stated is nowhere better exemplified than in the alliance between the Lombard towns and the papacy against the empire. But the cleric primarily sought the good of his own order. While he may have loved town liberty, he loved it in the way that the burgher loved that of the peasant. Indeed, the clergy sought freedom not only from princes but also from all lay dominance. The papacy fostered Lombard rebellions when combatting imperial prince-bishops. But it fought Rome's revolt in the mid-twelfth century, when Arnold of Brescia tried to do for Rome what Rome had done for Milan.

A significant movement related to the rise of town liberty during the eleventh and twelfth centuries was that of the Peace, the *Pax Dei* in its many aspects. This was an essentially ecclesiastical idea, and the institutions it created replaced the waning police of the devolving princely state. (*See Document No. 27.*) As a police agency, the

Peace mitigated social conflict. (*See Documents Nos. 9A, 37D.*) It was, therefore, of extraordinary significance in giving the European town the sense of social solidarity necessary for the success of its struggle for freedom. Like other vigorous and militant formulations of the *universitas*, the Genoese *compagna* of 1100 was a peace association. In France, the communes that fought for liberty described themselves as *communia pro pace*. (*See Document No. 34.*)

As Charles Petit-Dutaillis has shown, however, the northern French commune was anything but peaceful. The mere formation of a commune generally implied a revolutionary act. The same militant quality is observable elsewhere. The statutes of the Genoese *compagna* provide, for example, for the expansion of commerce and the domination of the Ligurian hinterland. As Augustine would describe it, the peace these citizens sought was not the one they already had but rather one more to their liking. Nîmes, Avignon, and Marseille obtained their liberties in the early thirteenth century, and abolished or restricted their princes by a religious confraternity and peace associations. The Peace, in short, was not divorced from revolution.

In conclusion, the late tenth through the first half of the thirteenth century was the age of the rise of the town and its liberty. Generally speaking, the degree of freedom from princely power was greater in southern than in northern Europe. In the north, the principal area was Flanders, although the Rhineland had much to boast about. Afterward, urban liberty continued to spread to the east and north, as is shown by the Hanseatic League. But it had already begun to wane in the mature centers of medieval town life.

— 5 —

THE AGE OF THE ARISTOCRACY

Where princes failed, an aristocracy was heir to their power. In Italy and Provence, this aristocracy comprised knights and businessmen rich enough to live nobly. The alignment was natural. Both groups were wealthy, one preeminently in land and the other in commerce. Both were suited to leadership. The knights were officers, commanding community defense and serving the prince's court. The burghers were leading entrepreneurs and merchants. Initially, however, they were separated by their orders. The eleventh century history of the Italian town was scarred by their battles. Milan's history illustrates the growth of an awareness of common interest that enabled its aristocracy to break the power of its princes. In 1037, the knights rose successfully against the prince-prelate and his captains. In 1044, the commoners rose against the knights and gained representation on the archbishop's council. From the mid-seventies, knights and commoners together attacked the princely office. Sometime between 1084 and 1097, a consulate appeared, opening the age of Milanese self-government. (*See Documents Nos. 7, 9A.*)

As we have seen, much the same often happened in the north, where towns had councils composed of knights and burghers. But the general pattern was different because of the division between knight and merchant, and town and country examined in the last chapter. Humble men certainly rose to lead in Italy, but participation in government by knights and rural magnates gave town society there a high tone from the start. Tall towers, veritable skyscrapers, were erected by knights and merchants to proclaim their prestige. Towers were built in the north also, but they were not so tall. Largely derived from the merchant settlement, the future patrician families were usually humbler and resisted the elegance and arrogance that mark aristocracy. Exceptions apart, Georges Espinas is right. The northern patricians who emblazoned their arms by the end of the thirteenth century were men whose origins were best left unsung.

Patrician origins remind us of the poor. In Italy, the rich served in the town militia as mounted knights. But there were also *pedites,* or footmen. (*See Documents Nos. 8, 37E, 46C.*) For Flanders, we have spoken about merchants, but have yet to see the humbler artisans. Yet poorer town elements participated in the movement against princely authority. Tumults bring everything to the surface. When Le Mans rose in 1070, one leader was named Stupid, another Three Balls. Lesser folk did not always direct their enmity against the prince. In Milan in 1044, the mass battled the knights. Princes made use of these divisions in order to retain command. In 1102, for example, the bishop and commons of Puy combined to tear down the proud towers of the knights "who were called minters." (*See Documents Nos. 9A, 10.*)

In general, however, the aristocracy mobilized the support of the people. It unified the town and fortified its community sense. Geographically, towns had often been divided between bishops and counts, not to speak of jurisdictions owned by viscounts, monasteries, and even simple knights. (*See Document No. 29.*) These were obliterated or weakened. Peace associations often insisted, moreover, that all townsmen were to be free. Ministerial or servile persons obviously served to reinforce the prince. The violent pogroms of Jews in the early crusading period were an aspect of the assault on ministerial groups. By this attack, however, quasi-servile artisan groups were united in equality with the whole. The use of the word burgher to replace merchant or *negociator* evidences an enlarged community sense. The word merchant generally meant what it said; burgher, however, meant both merchant and artisan. The reinvigorated idea of the *universitas,* then, served to advance the poor to legal equality. Moreover, the needs of an aristocracy seeking power and fearing the prince's use of town social division made it necessary to invite lesser social elements. Most peace statutes were promulgated with the consent of general assemblies of knights and *pedites,* of merchants and artisans.

Popular participation, even revolutionary democracy, was therefore part of urban political tradition. Real leadership, however, was always in, or fell into, the hands of the rich and aristocratic. The twelfth and thirteenth centuries witnessed the development of patrician political power. Patrician rule was rarely totally dominant, however, and it early displayed weaknesses. Plato long ago told us that divisions among the few permit the rise of the many. This truth is patent, but why the few who ruled the medieval town fell to feuding is less clear. A few conjectures are in order.

The patriciates of the twelfth century were not oligarchies. New families were admitted as they gained wealth. Later on, however, aristocracy became oligarchy.

By the late twelfth century in the south, and by the second half of the thirteenth in such northern areas as Flanders, new men found it harder to get in. Historians have proposed an economic reason for this process. Facing loss of wealth, the old aristocracy clung more tightly to office. Old exploitations declined and new developed: the landlord, for example, gave way before new men in commerce and industry. While useful, this analysis is insufficient. Landlords do not have to be rentiers: there was money in land and its produce for those who pushed. Besides, scions of good family often went into trade. Patrician families in thirteenth century Metz produced one great usurer after another. Generally, however, the established rich have different worlds to conquer than the new man coming up. His is that of the counting house; theirs, of elegance and governmental power. That is what the new man wants, but it is the end of the road for those who have it. Besides, money wealth cannot be retained, it can only be increased. For these reasons, a basic conflict among the few was that between those already in the patriciate and those equal or superior in wealth but excluded.

The struggle took many forms. Fearing the new and forgetting their own parents' practices, the old rich appealed to the poor by encouraging the condemnation of usury. The new answered by mobilizing popular support against tyrannous oligarchy. While some patrician scions found empire in supporting the cause of the new, the old families froze into office to hold the line. Rebellion disturbed the peace. In Italy, the office of the *potestas,* which we have seen in another context, was designed to mitigate these enmities. The *potestas* and his suite, were foreigners elected to govern the town, permitted no social or business life there. As much as possible, they were to be impartial arbiters maintaining the peace. (*See Documents Nos. 9B and C, 14, 36.*) In the long run, however, palliation was impossible and the struggle between the few prepared the way for the entry into government of the many during the mid- and later thirteenth century.

Patrician Government. In the aristocratic age, the medieval town was a republic. Its constitutional basis was the association of all male citizens, the *universitas.* Designed to maintain the peace, the *universitas* and its lead-

ing Good Men regulated and controlled the whole community by its elected officers. For this reason, it tried to
absorb or replace the old executive and judicial princely
court. Peace associations were initially promulgated by
the great and traditional public assemblies of the whole
citizenry. Commonly called Public Parliaments, these assemblies elected officers and approved statutes. Early in
their history, however, the Public Parliaments were
pushed into the background. Smaller councils of the El-
ders or the Wise, as they were called, replaced them in
practical management of affairs and election of officers.
In fact, as at Genoa, the initially elected college of consuls that ruled the town often became cooptative. (*See
Document No. 36.*)

Aristocratic government, however, preserved a democratic strain. Public parliaments retained restrictive power.
Although impeded by laws against demagogues, parliaments regularly and legally met. In Florence, the assembly
was called at least four times a year. Elsewhere such was
not the case, but everywhere constitutional change of
basic law required the multitude's approbation. Changes
of electoral procedure, new public and private law, taxes,
and war and peace traditionally composed basic law.
(*See Documents Nos. 36, 37A, B, and C.*) Moreover,
democracy was sometimes directly expressed, as at Nîmes
in 1198 where the whole people elected their consuls. We
note, however, that this particular edict was issued by a
prince. (*See Document No. 35.*) In 1207, when Nîmes
really gained freedom from its lord, the democratically
elected consulate was replaced by a cooptative body, half
of knights and half of burghers. (*See Document No. 9A
and B.*) This was not atypical, and reminds us of the
function of an aristocracy. A monopoly of office by those
whose wealth or status prevents them from being over-
awed or bought by the prince is essential for the development of republican institutions.

Nothing is more striking than the simplicity and informality of town government in the aristocratic age. Consuls served both as judges and executives. They and other
high officers were generally unpaid. Taxation was informal and undeveloped. We must not exaggerate, however.
In mature areas, as in Italy, judicial and executive functions were carefully distinguished. The *potestates* and

their specialist retinues were well paid. Moreover, specialization was everywhere growing as towns matured. But the picture drawn above defines the true character of the age. Henri Pirenne correctly said that this informality was aristocratic. Lack of specialization was not caused only by immaturity. It was also a reflection of the aristocrat's confidence that what he could not do was not worth doing anyway. By keeping higher offices unpaid, furthermore, he assured himself of their exercise. (*See Documents Nos. 36, 37A, B, and C.*)

In law, much the same qualities are evidenced. As we have seen, the idea of the *universitas* preached the equality of all citizens. Even where knights were important, their lawsuits with burghers were on an equal plane. For matters within their own order, however, knights frequently retained particular law that breached town unity. But particular law and reserved jurisdiction was rare in free towns because the town fathers tried to eradicate anything that divided the citizens. (*See Documents Nos. 121D and E.*) An example is seen in the abolition of the judicial duel. Although *pedites* were permitted this defense of their right in Mediterranean law, the duel reflected the military virtue of the knightly order. Moreover, its severity encouraged vendettas that could disturb peace. Finally, it offered an individual or family a way of minimizing the authority of the republic. By definition, the *universitas* insisted on its right to settle all major cases between citizens. (*See Documents Nos. 13, 23.*)

Community supremacy in law, however, should not be taken to imply that patricians fostered state omnipotence. True, the introduction of Roman jurisprudence from the late eleventh century enhanced state prerogative. This development, however, was slowed by several factors related to the aristocratic tenor of the age. The subtleties of Roman law indeed inspired specialization. But this was tempered by a jurist school that preached simplicity and clarity. Again, Rome's statist principles were mitigated by the Glossators who harmonized them with current custom. Lastly, it was characteristic of the age that most civil suits were settled by private arbitration, lighly supervised by town authority. The aristocracy was the heir of its prejudice. Having fought the state belonging to the prince, it suspected it even when it owned it itself.

The aspect of Roman law that appealed to townsmen was not its statism. The revival of learned studies in Roman jurisprudence was the work of the eleventh century in Italy. It culminated in the creation of the *studium* at Bologna, and thence spread slowly throughout Europe. Like the contemporary movement of the Peace, one of its functions was to substitute for the old common government of the empire. When the Italian republics shattered imperial power, they required a new legal *koiné* to make communication among themselves possible. Besides, Roman law was called upon for another reason. As we have seen, the old princely state used ecclesiastics as its jurists and scribes. Even in tenth and eleventh century Italy, where lay literacy remained firmer than in the ruder north, most judges and notaries about whom we have specific knowledge were churchmen. When the clergy fought for freedom from the secular state, however, they were obliged to—indeed, they wished to—surrender offices that made them responsible to lay authority. Moreover, their design was aided by the need for specialization of a maturing society. In a village, a priest could double as a lawyer. In town, he would not have time. For these reasons, the eleventh and twelfth centuries saw the slow rebirth of lay literacy and legal culture. In the mature Mediterranean, this process was well advanced by the end of the twelfth century. Elsewhere, it took longer, a comparable stage being attained only during the thirteenth century, sometimes much later.

The results were twofold, institutional and ideological. A secular notariate and legal profession appeared, ending the old ecclesiastical monopoly of literacy. Roman law was the textbook of lay legal culture. More than that, it was an ethical system, implicitly subjecting ecclesiastical to lay authority. The secularization of law is therefore part of the rebirth of lay literacy and lay ethics that together define secularism. (*See Documents Nos. 14A, and 48.*) It is worth emphasizing, however, that townsmen were not the only pioneers. Secularism was the work of all society. It was not the consuls of Milan who combined the ancient image of the king-priest with the newer themes of Bolognese Roman law to found the militant secularism of the future. That was Frederick II, emperor and lord of southern Italy.

Social Ideals. A description of the aristocratic age would be incomplete without treating those social ideals always known to man but that find a pertinent formulation peculiar to each period. The idea of liberty was a mark of this period. Charters reminded their readers that freedom was man's natural state from which some had fallen through sin. They urged man to restore his fellows to their prior condition. Great intellectuals, largely clerical, elaborated ancient historical schemes wherein ever better ages followed one another to culminate in a terrestrial paradise preparing the way for eternal bliss. The final age was conceived as one in which labor was lightened by love, law replaced by brotherhood, all announced by man's conquest of nature. Technology would exploit nature external to man. Nature within man, the Old Adam, was to be subjected by reason. Indeed, liberty involved man in more than begging for tax reduction. It bound his conscience to the search for brotherhood.

The consciences of the rich and powerful were deeply touched in this age. We do not say, of course, that there were none who stopped at nothing to get lucre. Georges Espinas has told the story of John Boine Broke, a veritable industrial robber baron. But social censure awakens most consciences and obliges man to shun excessive gain. In social terms, usury was the crime of those who consistently sought immoderate profit, thereby becoming notorious. The usurer's enemies in the medieval town were those whose wealth was that of the rentier and the poor who stood to lose by exploitative entrepreneurial power. True, both groups were themselves inclined to immoderacy. That of the rentier was, as we have seen, political tyranny. The poor were the most usurious of all, said the preacher, preserved for virtue only because they lacked the means to live viciously.

These social pressures abated excess and encouraged legislation to protect the many from exploitation by the few. What gave consistency to local authority was the church. Admittedly, clergy were businessmen or occasionally even usurers. But business was not the church's work: it was busy elsewhere. The church was the greatest rentier of all, and was therefore hostile to new men and business methods that ruined old and predictable arrangements. We do not mean, however, that all churchmen attacked trading. The greatest late thirteenth century scholastics, Aquinas and Scotus, saw in commerce a licit service to the commonwealth and stated that the merchants' labor and risk deserved remuneration. Their more popularly read peer, Giles of Rome, went even further. As the soldier for his fighting, he said, each craft was worthy of its hire. He specifically stated that a merchant could profit from his knowledge of market conditions.

Moderation aside, however, religious rigorism condemned all usury, all lending at interest: "Lend, and seek no gain therefrom." This is not a question of limiting economic excessiveness such as described above. It is a total conception, and it is therefore worthwhile to seek why the church took and maintained this extraordinary position. One reason was that churchmen were an order, jealous and proud. They queried the salvation of those in trade as they doubted that of those who lived by the sword. The church derived its empire from the needs of man's conscience. There is no darker bruise upon that part of man than that left by usury, for it destroys brotherhood. As an order, then, the church consistently condemned usury.

Again, Benjamin N. Nelson has reminded us that the church extended to Christian society an ancient Jewish tribal brotherhood within which usury, like slavery, was forbidden. There is, therefore, more than order jealousy and function here. The prohibition of usury was a definition of the religion itself. At first sight, however, we are faced by a seeming contradiction. Church legislation always asserted the great principle, but, almost into the twelfth century, little was done about enforcement, save for the self-discipline of the clergy itself. It was only later, from the late twelfth century to the early fourteenth century, that specific legislation and wide popular polemic attacked usurers in a practical way. This contradiction, however, is easily resolved. We have seen how late Rome and its princely heirs legislated to protect the many against the few. Confessedly, secular law did not satisfy the rigorist: Roman law permitted interest. But, while the state was senior partner, the church was not in the position to do more than grumble. (*See Documents Nos. 55, 56.*)

The weakening of the princely state changed the picture.

An age of something like entrepreneurial liberty or economic individualism ensued, but society soon summoned the church to replace the state. The peace of God and the Crusade were early stimulants for church intervention. Peace within and the protection of soldiers who fought without required the regulation of debt. Indeed, Christendom was the brotherhood that the church protected. The actual enforcement of church legislation, however, fell short of rigorist ideals. The obvious impracticality of the ideal of brotherhood made concession necessary. Besides, those who conspired to mitigate the severity of ecclesiastical injunctions had a profound ethical argument. An insistence that others should strive toward the unattainable is the usury that religious men customarily exact from the rest of mankind. The church bowed to the practical world by developing conceptions of risk that eased austerity. Besides, a bad debtor was considered almost as anathema as a wicked creditor.

The effect of these conceptions is not to be judged by the numbers of unlucky usurers caught by ecclesiastical police. The important thing was the growth of means to placate society by restoring to it a portion of the gains made. One way was formal testamentary restitution either directly to those from whom usury had been wrung or to charity generally. To rigorists, philanthropy, or restitution during an unreformed lifetime, was deceptive. Nevertheless, philanthropy rivaled restitution in creating charitable institutions.

Part of the money won back for society went into schooling. We have already seen the rise of lay literacy in this age: the clergy were Europe's first teachers. Starting with simple and undifferentiated parish and chapter schools in the early eleventh century, a more complex and more laic educational system appeared. (*See Document No. 4.*) A distinction between elementary and secondary schools is found in the thirteenth century in towns as far apart as Ypres and Florence. While provoking town-gown conflicts, the development of the universities, particularly of the secular faculties of law and medicine, is well known and encouraged a healthy rivalry between educational institutions and towns. Education was largely financed by charity.

More impressive was the growth of medical and

charitable services. Again, the roots of later development were gate charities and hospitals of monasteries and cathedral chapters. Leprosaries built along monastic lines, hospices, hospitals for general purposes, for the aged poor, for eye and skin diseases, and lying in wards are examples of hospital work. (*See Documents Nos. 4, 14B and C.*) Hospital orders proliferated: the Hospitallers of the twelfth, for example, and the Trinitarians of the thirteenth century. In both Italy and southern France, this latter time witnessed the beginnings of the secularization of these facilities. The rich man had been summoned to aid the poor by his endowments. His was a religious duty: the *pauper* was the Christ.

The Gilds. Humble men often find that, while it is pleasant to be helped, it is more profitable to help oneself. Moreover, those who are individually weak and who share the hope of being strong collectively tend to work together. It is in this sense that we introduce the gild, the means whereby the lesser stood against the greater. The medieval gild has a double origin: Mediterranean and mature, northern and primitive.

Exemplified by the Pavian Book of Honors of c.1010, the first references to Italian and other Mediterranean gilds evidence an advanced social articulation. The merchant gild does not constitute the only corporation. Other specialties are also organized. Moreover, duty to the commonwealth was particularly emphasized. Exceptions apart, most early Italian gild statutes deal with economic matters. Social work and brotherly camaraderie already found their place in special institutions, particularly in parish confraternities, or *caritates*. Other than service, the corporations enjoyed no exercise of state power. In fact, princely law spoke indifferently of the magistracy (*magisterium*) or the ministry (*ministerium*) of a profession, stressing its privileges and duties. In short, though simplified, these bodies inherited the tradition of Rome's *collegia*. (*See Document No. 47.*)

The early medieval northern gild was different: it lacked specialization. The gild merchant of the German tenth century combined hospitality, social work, defense, and trade. It was a blood brotherhood of warrior merchants, derived from tribal society. In effect, also, the gild governed the merchants' *Wik*, a practice that marked the institutions of lightly urbanized areas such as England even through the twelfth century. As society matured, however, the northern gild came closer to the Mediterranean corporation. Moreover, the evolution of the northern gild illustrates a pattern characteristic of medieval corporatism. During the late eleventh and early twelfth centuries, northern town government usually separated from the gild merchant. At that time, also, the first real artisan gilds appear. As society grows, its institutions split, becoming more articulated. In the early thirteenth century, one association governed the Toulousan cloth industry. Barely a century later, it was ruled by at least five. (*See Document No. 50.*)

Growing specialization, then, made new gilds possible. What made them necessary, however, was the system of enterprise. We have already noted that technology made the domestic system feasible for larger industry. The textile industry was capitalized by partnerships: the entrepreneur contributing capital and the artisan labor. The small artisan clearly needed protection against the large entrepreneur if he was to receive a fair part of the profit. Moreover, twelfth and early thirteenth century statutes advantaged the entrepreneur or the one who supplied raw materials. He was the *dominus,* and the artisan was often prohibited from fixing prices and limiting competition in his profession. (*See Document No. 50.*) The organization of artisans and smaller entrepreneurs, however, set a limit to abuse.

The ideal gildsman was both artisan and entrepreneur. He worked with his hands but enjoyed some ownership or control over means of production. There was nothing restful about this, however. The gild structure had to keep growing to keep the balance between the entrepreneur and artisan. Older or more general gilds in the cloth industry either became or were founded as entrepreneurial associations. Middling gilds, such as shoemakers, came closest to the ideal. Lower gilds, usually newer, were workers' organizations. The reason for the need of expansion was the way in which the little artisan or businessman protected himself against the rich: by his monopoly of the right to work in a certain profession. Gildsmen not only fought the rich, therefore, they also battled the poor who tried to get in. There was brotherhood here, but there was also fratricide.

The twelfth and thirteenth centuries saw the first age of expanding corporationalism in urban economic life. Its results were spectacular. By the mid-thirteenth century, Paris had 101 gilds. Hours and wages were regulated: night work was prohibited in all but 18 gilds. By the early fourteenth century, the Saturday half-holiday had been accepted and holy days had so multiplied that the industrial work week in Artois sank to four days—long days, from sunup to sundown. Holidays remind us that the church was instrumental in this amelioration. Not all of the church, be it understood. Bishops, for example, often fought for the rich. But the mission preached by the new orders of the friars generally favored the extension of economic corporations. (*See Document No. 52.*) The church also sponsored the confraternities that provided basic social services: burial expenses, marriage gifts, for example, and sickness compensation.

Another basic aspect of the medieval gild was its aggressiveness, what Gunnar Mickwitz has called its "cartelfunction." Its monopoly tendency naturally offended the consumer. Moreover, the gild's interest in local small industry also harmed the mercantile aristocracy engaged in export and import. These interests combined to forbid gild monopoly and restraint of trade. (*See Document No. 50.*) They were not sufficiently powerful, however, to arrest gild development. Important institutions aided the gilds. We have already mentioned the role of the church. It seems evident, also, that princes advanced gild interests. Despite the more matured economy of early thirteenth century Italy, gilds there were not much more developed than those in northern Europe. The textile town of Douai had practically no artisan gilds of any significance by the mid-century. Paris had over a hundred. What explains these contrasts? Douai was a free town, ruled by an entrepreneurial patriciate. Italy's republics were governed by similar elements. Paris is our key: the north retained a stronger image of princely state power. Northern princes fostered artisan corporations to weaken the independence of urban aristocracies. (*See Documents Nos. 47-49, 51.*)

These considerations remind us of the link between economic and political power. Another function of gild aggression was to implement the entry of middling and lesser social elements into political life. Lacking leisure and wealth, little men individually were not strong enough to impress their will on government, nor were they in position to hold office regularly. Gild political activity provided a way in which they could find real representation in government. The first Italian evidences of this participation derive from the very late twelfth and early thirteenth centuries. Princely Montpellier was well ahead: her gild organization was fused with municipal government by 1204.

Occasional social conflict aside, the twelfth and thirteenth centuries were the great age of the medieval town. Better than many words, a few figures will illustrate the social elements, and the provision of legal, social, and religious services in the town. The examples are chosen from the area between the extremes of north and south and represent the small to middling urbanism characteristic of the middle ages.

In 1262, Toulouse had a population of 20 to 25,000 souls. It boasted 5 hospices for clergy, 5 *resclusanie* or homes for unmarried women, 7 leprosaries, and 13 hospitals. One hospital contained 56 beds, another was probably larger, most looked after around 13 aged.

In 1304, the population of Carcassonne was estimated at about 9,500. There were 43 noble households, 12 Lombard, and 30 Jewish. Law and government were represented by 63 notaries, 15 advocates, and 40 soldiers, police, and messengers. Health, religion, and charity were served by 9 university trained doctors, 9 priests, and 250 clergy.

— 6 —

CRISIS AND REPAIR

The late middle ages was a time of troubles. This was not anticipated by men in the late thirteenth or early fourteenth centuries. Charters expressed the conviction that town liberty and prosperity would continue to grow.

This hope was traduced. Again, as all who saw affirmed, town population increased astonishingly at the turn of the centuries. The fathers planned enlarged walled enclosure to receive the expected expansion. In not a few cases, the new walls were not filled until the eighteenth century. Anticipation had lost touch with reality.

The crisis had many aspects. Several derived from factors outside western society itself. A cycle of sickness afflicted Europe from before the mid-fourteenth century Black Plague. More significant perhaps, though less immediately catastrophic, was the rise of non-western power. An example was the assault on Europe by a revived Islam. The Moslems reacted vigorously to their defeat in the twelfth century. They had already begun to gain ground, when, in the thirteenth century, they were thrown back by the Mongols. Momentarily unifying Asia, these pagans saved the day for the Latins. From the mid-fourteenth century, however, Chinese resistance and the liberation of Iran weakened the great khan's empire and assured the subjection of the Latins in the Near East. From this time, Islam moved forward as the Ottoman slowly mobilized and subjected the Near East, Balkans, and Africa. The Turks were heir to both Islam and Byzantium. The fall of Constantinople in 1453, the absorption of Egypt in 1517, and the siege of Vienna in 1529 mark the apogee of Moslem power. Its attraction was almost irresistible. As late as 1630, it was suggested that the Capuchin missions be withdrawn lest the fathers turn Turk.

Warfare and Society. External stimulus, however, does not explain the crisis. Historians have noted that depopulation was not wholly due to the sickness of the age. Some of the ailments were themselves profoundly psychological, such as the dancing plagues of St. Vitus. Moreover, there is evidence that towns continued to decline even when sickness was not rife. Some areas were afflicted by the plague but by nothing else, and soon recouped their losses. Even at peak, furthermore, the area under Turkish power was not comparable to Europe in population or technology. In fact, Europeans deserted to Islam because of opportunities for technicians there. Emigrant Spanish Jews built Turkish field artillery on the French model. Moreover, when we look within the west itself we perceive that the world turned upside-down in the late middle ages. Until the early thirteenth century, England had always been invaded by the French, and, until the fourteenth, Scotland by the English. That is as it should be: twenty million French outnumbered three million English. And as for those barelegged Scots . . . ! Later, it all reversed. The English fell on the French, the Scots on the English, and both enjoyed astonishing success for a time. To employ another example: once, . . . as shown by castramentation and local militias, defense ruled war. (*See Document No. 8.*) Then, attack won the day. Cannon and foreign mercenaries dominated battlefield and siege in the late middle ages.

Perhaps the clearest indication that something was wrong was the evolution of the Crusade. In the past, the Crusade mobilized Latins to conquer foreigners. By the thirteenth century, this institution was widely questioned. Missions were developed; pagans were thought to have natural rights. The savagery of the earlier idea had been softened. Along with this, however, went something else: the Crusade had fallen back into Europe. The attacks on Byzantine schismatics in 1204, on Albigensian heretics in 1209, were the beginnings of the use of the Crusade by popes and princes against enemies at home. In fact, the French became so habituated to raising the Crusade tithe for their wars that they almost declared a pope heretical for seeking to withhold it.

The internalizing of the Crusade shows that war outside had become war within. Until the fifteenth century, and sometimes even after, war developed a breath-taking vehemence lacking in earlier ages. Moreover, wars between sovereign powers were not the only instances of violence and disaggregation. Social warfare was endemic in late medieval society: a cycle of revolutions and social troubles began in the latter thirteenth century and continued into the beginning of the fifteenth century in Italy and France. From there, it spread to adjacent regions. Admittedly, there had been revolutions before. When urban liberty had been proclaimed in the late eleventh and early twelfth centuries, society had been deeply disturbed. Moreover, that early age was marked by severe economic dislocation. But there is a clear distinction between that time of crisis and the later one. Before, towns won liberty and their populations increased. Later, towns lost liberty and their populations decreased.

Social war was the order of the day and was reflected in ideology. We have already seen that ideas about the perfect society and brotherhood were widely current in the medieval age. Late medieval man developed these arguments with unprecedented intensity and publicity. Preachers urged their audiences to abolish the division into mine and thine that was the source of all evil, reminding them that to hold everything in common restored paradise. This mission explains why revolutionaries such as the Florentine *Ciompi* of 1378 thought of themselves as "God's people." Of course, these were not new dreams: they were part of the western religious tradition. But the peculiarity of late medieval man was that he insisted on confusing the way it is with the way it ought to be. His madness lay in trying to make his dreams come true.

The conflict between town and countryside was also reinvigorated in this age. Old illusions were shattered and relationships embittered. When Bologna granted the peasants in her republic citizenship and liberty from their lords in 1257, the end of an age was signaled. The peasants were free. Once seignorial jurisdiction was destroyed, however, the villages were open to town exploitation. In fact, the food-hungry towns of northern Italy often granted an ineffectual citizenship or freedom to peasants in exchange for producing strictly regulated crops to be sold at fixed prices. The villager had lost an old master to become the slave of the town.

Moreover, villages were no longer what they had been in the past. We have seen how the earlier medieval period was marked by the relatively greater growth of the town than the countryside. In the late middle ages, this process often reversed. Villages became little towns and their governments were urbanized. An early example is the Lauragais outside of Toulouse's walls. In the early thirteenth century, this area boasted no village free of seignorial domination. By 1271, ninety-six villages elected their consuls and shared government with their seignors. Villagers feared their seignors but little: the enemy was exploitative Toulouse. In fact, the countryside had begun to react against town dominance. Throughout the late middle ages,

Flemish towns tried to prevent the development of rural industry with some success. Even in this highly urbanized area, however, rural society fought back. Its principal agency was a revived princely state that reduced town liberty. Its achievement was the rise of the rural *Franc* of Bruges to equality in the Flemish estates with the great towns, Bruges, Ghent, and Ypres.

Economy and Population.   There is only one other principal manifestation of this crisis that needs to be discussed. In France and Italy, mature parts of Europe, for example, population grew into the early fourteenth century. This may be transcribed in other terms. Economic life was characterized then by maximum utilization of the land, indeed, of all facilities urban or rural. Even in mountain areas such as the Dauphiné and Pyrenees steps were taken to preserve remaining forests. The frontier, it seemed, had been filled up. But nature seldom imposes absolute limits to man's increase: Europe later supported greater numbers than in the medieval age. A growing technology could have answered the problem.

Although the late middle ages saw some very significant inventions, they were not evident during the early part of the crisis. They appeared during it, not in time to prevent it. Social organization seems related to this fact. During the early troubles, a maximum subdivision of property together with an anticipation of high reward for services seem to have been general. The results of this seem to have been unhappy. A difficulty to mobilize for common purposes was represented by interminable lawsuits. For a time, rural exploitations morcellated to a point where they became incapable of implementing technological change on a scale commensurate with society's needs. Henri Pirenne has pointed out how the rise of artisan gilds tended to revive urban economic autarky and slow the development of long-range commerce.

While this congealment was in the making, its cure began to appear. If land and town had been overcrowded, they now became deserted. The experience of Toulouse is typical. From 1410 to 1443, its citizens underwent six severe famines, six epidemics or plagues, eight great fires or floods, twenty years of warfare and banditry, and two important social revolts. Of four bridges at the end of the thirteenth century, only one remained. The suburbs vanished; the population sank by a full third. In general, the areas most affected were the populous and well-developed parts of Europe. These regions only began to revive again in the fifteenth century, from the end of the first quarter or first half. Other districts were more fortunate for a time. Eastern and northern Germany flourished throughout most of the fourteenth century, and only caught the malaise seriously during the fifteenth. Some areas escaped all but the plague: the Netherlands being the lucky example. The semi-desertion of town and countryside is perhaps the most dramatic example of the erasure or rationalizing of property and other rights in the west. Nature herself seemed determined to wipe the board clean and give man a new start.

This rationalization made possible the erection of larger units of exploitation. And what was made possible by this inadvertent process was made necessary by the competitive and martial nature of the age. Neither the old seignory nor localist town was suited to hold its own in the fourteenth and fifteenth centuries. Indeed, their desire to do so inspired the many revolutions and wars. Province-wide interests gradually produced new regional specialties and linked town and countryside. An example is the fourteenth and fifteenth century development of Armagnac in southern France as an export center for wool and wine. Old seignorial families were obliterated or subordinated to the greater Armagnac dynasty and towns lost their liberties. This was "feudal concentration" with a vengeance for the good of the Armagnac line, but it also benefited the province.

Indeed, the emergence of provincial dynasties was typical of France during the Hundred Years War. During that agony, France split up into quasi-independent segments. The older French localist traditions had resisted the precocious centralism imposed by the kings at the turn of the thirteenth and fourteenth centuries, and destroyed France. The promise of this separatism, however, was evinced by the mobilizing of whole provinces into effective unity. Before the Hundred Years War, there had been seignories and towns, and the king. After, there was the king and his provinces. Provincial separatism was a stage in the development of the nation.

As it stands, our description of the late middle ages

seems unfaithful to what we know of the history of town
life. Early fifteenth century north Italy exhibited great
towns: Venice, Milan, Florence, Genoa, to name the most
outstanding. Around 1500, the population of Paris had
risen about three times over its medieval apogee two
centuries before. But, before we draw any conclusions,
we should remember that the population of France as
a whole had perhaps slightly declined in the same period,
despite the fifteenth century lift. In the mid-thirteenth
century, furthermore, Florence, Pisa, and Siena were
more or less on a par. Two centuries later, Pisa and
Siena were decisively smaller and weaker than their
neighbor. These examples show that large towns either
remained stable during the time of troubles or even grew.
Middling towns, the typical range of earlier medieval
urbanism, clearly shrank. When we remember that many
villages seem to have done better, we perceive a shift
of momentous magnitude. While everything had declined
in one sense, in another, urbanism had matured. It had
reached a new and higher base or step for future development in the modern era.

   The Corporations.   The capacity to concentrate resources and human energy in larger units is also shown
within the towns themselves. In France, for example, gilds
multiplied during the thirteenth and early fourteenth centuries. The general collapse slowed the expansion, but it
picked up again in the mid-fifteenth century. That century and the beginning of the next witnessed the maximum
increase in the creation of gilds. And, as Gunnar Mickwitz has proposed, the greatest number of gilds was
attained well in the modern period, in the era of Louis
XIV. In fact, the gild structure had so expanded that the
term gild does not suffice to describe it. A general system
of corporatism had replaced the older and simpler form.

   Corporatism became the townsman's way of life during
the late middle ages. Corporations embraced every type
of urban activity: entrepreneurial, artisan, shopkeeper,
professional, and official, such as notaries and judges.
Moreover, artisan gilds split into associations of masters
as against those of workers. Naturally, this was partly the
result of the perennial effort of gild masters to monopolize
their craft and to limit membership. But this drive was
countered, as we shall see, by an enterprising and regula-

tive state—at least, during the medieval period. What the split really portends is that the working force of well-developed industries split into two groups: one with capital and managerial experience and another with little to offer but their arms—*brassiers,* as they said in France. The late fourteenth and still more the fifteenth centuries, therefore, saw journeymen organize associations. Stiff resistance by the masters slowed this movement, but progress was made. Labor sometimes brigaded within the old gilds. Sometimes, as at Strasbourg, independent bodies were sponsored by state authority. Lastly, the shape-up system was regulated by both state and gild for mutual benefit, and parish and other associations sprang up to provide necessary social services. (*See Documents Nos. 51-53.*)

Corporation growth may seem to indicate a multiplication of rights to labor and profession that might inhibit economic growth and the introduction of technical innovation. That this was a tendency, there is no doubt, and it eventually became a real problem of Mediterranean economy in the modern age. For the period discussed here, however, this tendency was offset by the rapid growth of new corporations. Here was not a congealing of old right but rather the creation of new enterprise. Besides, the state intervened to prevent corporate constriction of the economy. It is worth pausing here to examine the gild's relation to the state.

For reasons discussed before, thirteenth and fourteenth century gilds tried to enter government. The evolution of the Florentine constitution is a classic example. By 1250, the greater gilds, entrepreneurial or professional, pushed the old aristocracy down. In the eighties and nineties, the middle gilds of artisans and shopkeepers moved toward power. Throughout the next century, workers' gilds, such as the carders, or *Ciompi,* tried to enter political life. For a while, then, the state was almost captured by professional and trade corporations. Town legislation sometimes even excluded from office those who did not work with their hands. (*See Documents Nos. 9A, 36, 40A.*)

Several factors, however, diminished gild strength. First, the multiplication of gilds decentralized their political power. The textile *Lana* gildsmen in Florence were businessmen able to mobilize a whole industry for the early advancement of the popular party. No matter how numerous or militant they were, the *Ciompi* were only one part of that industry. Movements such as theirs rarely gained power, though that happened occasionally. Their real effect was to so subdivide an industry that it could no longer act with political efficacy. Second, the importance of the corporation in economic and political life made external regulation necessary. Most gild statutes were proposed by gildsmen but published by state authority, a prince's privilege or the consent of a Public Parliament. State power over the gilds increased throughout the later middle ages. (*See Documents Nos. 46D, 50.*) It often insisted on night work, induction of new masters, and upon innovations in technique. In France, for example, the introduction of printing is a study of state coercion and accommodation of craft interests. Moreover, the state always had the last word: it spoke for the common good and could enlist the public against corporate particularism. Given government regulation, then, the development of the corporations was another way by which society was mobilized for common purposes and developed a degree of specialization unknown before.

Social Invention. The warlike difficulties of the age stimulated invention. Business institutions enlarged and became more permanent. Although *sui generis*, Genoese *Maona* are a case in point. They were capitalized on a greater scale than previous enterprise. The *Maona* of Chios-Phocea of 1346 issued no less than 2,013 shares. *Maona* were state chartered, and the close relation of state and corporation implied control and investment guarantee. Investors were liable only up to the sum of their investment. Unlike old private partnerships, *Maona* were not usually created for short terms. They reflected the perpetuity inherent in the state. Lastly, they embraced a wider range of activities. The Chios *Maona*, for example, not only exploited economic enterprise in the Aegean area but also exercised the power of coercion and police in lieu of the state. When we add to the *Maona* the state-owned military and merchant flotillas of Venice, we see the initial form of the Iberian *flota* and northern companies that exploited the New World's seas and opened the routes to the east at the dawn of modern times.

If great Genoa produced agencies enabling it to withstand Mediterranean militarism and competitiveness, the milling industry of backward Toulouse showed equal inventiveness in the face of disaster. In the late thirteenth century, there were three important mill associations on the Garonne river. By the mid-fifteenth century, there were only two, one of them much reduced. During the crisis, these associations had evolved spectacularly. From being narrow bodies of mill operators and owners, they became broad associations of shareholders in a common enterprise. The shareholders entrusted the operation of the mills to well paid specialists, workers and officers. Later, a real managerial group appeared, specializing in legal and financial affairs. Management developed the conception of the *honor* to describe the society as a whole. Similar to a modern corporation, the *honor* was a fictional legal person, theoretically perpetual. Its investors were liable only up to the amount invested. In a local mill industry, the crisis had produced a form—albeit incomplete —of the modern corporation.

Banking underwent much the same transformation. During the crisis, it suffered severely from crashes. Florentine banking and merchant interests had been shaken as early as 1282. Intermittent crises built up to a grand collapse in 1347 when the famous Bardi and Peruzzi firms went down the drain. The reconstruction of the Florentine system was signaled by the rise of the Medici. Their enterprise differed from that of their predecessors. It was not a single family firm like the Peruzzi, but rather an interlocking system of partnerships bringing in much more capital and sharing the risk more widely. Furthermore, the Medici political role connected their commerical and banking empire with the Florentine state. Theirs was not, therefore, a simple private enterprise. In effect, it was an expression of Florentine public credit and state policy.

State intervention was true of banking in general. Government was everywhere invited to guarantee deposits, and, in return, regulated banking. In Venice, for example, it controlled the credit creation of private overdraft banks by requiring them, in effect, to have a regulated percentage of their assets in specie. Bankers were not allowed to speculate in commodities directly. In effect, also, banks were obliged to buy shares of the state debt.

At first glance, these regulations were reactionary and inhibited free credit expansion. On the other hand, they made real bankers by stimulating specialization in function. Furthermore, the requirement that banks carry part of the state debt illustrates again the mobilization of capital for common effort characteristic of the fourteenth and fifteenth centuries.

To conclude, the organizing basis of commerce and industry in the late middle ages was the corporation: the gild, the Toulouse *honor,* the Genoese *Maona,* and, most of all, the corporation sole, the state. Moreover, as we already know, the corporate idea was clearly connected to that of brotherhood. In the eye of the church, corporate gain was more licit than that of an individual. Corporatism has its own ethic, and it has a palpable superiority to that of the economic individual. It seeks the common good directly.

Oddly, corporatism engendered its opposite, the heroic individual. The annals of the time record the histories of lively and turbulent entrepreneurs: Jacques Coeur, Francis Coppola of Naples, and others. These meteoric figures accumulated huge fortunes and discovered new directions for industry and commerce. All were closely connected to the state, as financiers and officers. Their careers, however, were haunted by the hostility of the gildsmen. Their function was interstitial: they related groups of corporations together, and they worked in the murky area outside the corporations altogether. These were the regions of the economy that were not yet protected by gild statutes or those that could never be honestly nor publicly marshalled into a corporate structure. This was their heroism: they were always on the frontier, looking for something new. This was also their crime: they were the blackmarketeers, the sellers of favors, the grand usurers. Many ended their lives stripped of wealth or even on the block. Ironically, their deaths had an economic function too: their wealth ended in the prince's treasury. Their lives served to mobilize otherwise unobtainable capital and social energy for the good of the commonwealth.

What was true of these grand viziers of public finance and enterprise was also true of a variety of social groups in late medieval life. Some were privileged by the state to lend at interest. Such were, for example, those who exercised the Lombard privilege in the Germanies. A most important group was the Jews. Late thirteenth and early fourteenth century popular movements had seen them expelled from England, most of France, and severely wounded in other parts of Europe. Elsewhere they continued to flourish, although increasingly subjected to and generally impoverished by hostile populations. While, as in Castile, some Jewish communities boasted individuals of great wealth and local presidency, most were poor. The Jew was reduced to serve as a petty usurer, artisan, or shopkeeper. The repetitive cycle of life experienced by Jewish and occasional Christian communities serving similar functions was surprisingly like the history of a Jacques Coeur. An era of privilege and relative affluence, provoking growing popular hostility, culminated in expropriation and temporary expulsion by the prince. The function was the same, also: concentrating capital from the interstices of a corporate society.

In conclusion, the malady which Europe experienced in the fourteenth and early fifteenth centuries left its trace in vacant fields and deserted towns. After the crisis, western man was probably not as well off, and certainly not as innocent, as he had been before. But he had laid the foundations for a new and greater age. He had enlarged the unit of enterprise and industry. He was about to enlarge his world. The development of the state and of the nation were decisive stages in mobilizing man's social energy. They were buttressed by an elaborate corporate structure that, marked by real coercion and deep suffering, concentrated wealth and energy in a way undreamed of in the earlier medieval period. These were the agencies that gave Europe a new world: that of the cannon, of the sailing vessel, of the printing press. The regulated use of these innovations made Europe's conquest of the globe possible.

THE PRINCE AND THE PEOPLE

During the late middle ages, aristocratic republicanism collapsed and town government generally became princely or monarchical. A reason for this was the warlike character of the era. Hasty emergency requires command, and that is best exercised by one. The importance of this development is two-fold. First, the martial prince became the agency to project outside the town or society itself energies and passions that could find no release within save at the cost of the body social. Princely militarism was decisive in the development of the northern nation-state and the Italian town-state at the edge of modern times. The Florentine Machiavelli admired the warrior prince Castruccio Castracani. In fact, historians have sometimes viewed the rise of the Italian prince as the emergence of an office specialized in war and diplomacy. Second, the evolution of the prince's warlike glory was a stage in Europe's secularization. In the earlier medieval period, the ecclesiastical Crusade served the same function on an oecumenical level. With the failure of this idea, a lay agency assumed its office and developed the thirst for war that led to Europe's conquests.

We have seen how the Crusade was balanced by the Peace of God: peace at home, war abroad. In smaller compass, what was true of the church was true of the state. As the church was above party and particular interest, so also was the prince. Impartiality was his policy, his police with which to arbitrate social conflict. The monarch's impartiality derived from self-interest. His was the estate princely, and he belonged to no other. Everywhere displayed by princes, self-interest and opportunism constitute the best definition of monarchy. Where towns were strong, as in Italy, for example, princes rose by using the discontent of the exploited countryside.

Whichever way the prince turned his favor, however, to town or countryside, his action bound together a whole region or, as in the north, a nation. (*See Document No. 46.*) The rise of the prince was the political parallel to the economic concentration examined in our previous chapter.

Princely impartiality, however, was not unimpeded. The conception of the nation shows this. Ideally, princely power evolves toward universality, as that of the people toward localism. Few princes rejected the government of provinces because their inhabitants spoke another language. None refused to employ foreign soldiers. The replacement of local militias by professional and partly foreign armies testifies to princely impartiality. Local interests and inhibitions imposed on the prince by his teachers, however, prevented the realization of the ideal. Despite this, the rise of princes and kings mobilized Europe into larger units. Even Italy had fewer states in 1550 than in 1250. Moreover, although in miniature, the systematic constitutions of the Italian states mirrored the idea of centralism more perfectly than did those of the larger northern nations.

The political evolution of north and central Italy is the most important for the historian of urbanism. Elsewhere monarchs were there to begin with: their power had only to be amplified. Italy's peculiarity is that republican towns themselves created princely government. Moreover, all but the final stages of the translation from republicanism to monarchy was accomplished without any significant pressure from outside. This teaches the historian that urban man is not necessarily republican. He has sometimes found the rule of princes to be the best solution to his problems. In short, there is no one necessary political form for town life.

Democracy. The twelfth century Italian town constitution was aristocratic. It evolved toward democracy during the thirteenth and early fourteenth centuries. Italian urbanism then came as near to rule by the many as any highly evolved and male dominated society is ever likely to be. Basic power was usually exercised by a council of Ancients chosen by a variety of electoral bodies and methods. First were the corporations, professional, entrepreneurial, artisan, and shopkeeper. Second came the militia companies comprising all male inhabitants. Third, council seats were equally divided between each quarter of the town. This system therefore mixed corporate and geographical methods of representation. Councilmen were chosen by a combination of lot and vote. (*See Document No. 9D, E, and F.*)

There were limits to the degree of real democracy within these constitutions. Women participated little in government, as indeed they rarely did anywhere from prehistoric and tribal ages to the industrial revolution. To use the analogy of northern European experience in this time, what little role they played was through the gilds in which they worked or in which, as widows, they served as guardians of their children's rights or heirs of their husbands'. Women did not hold town political office—save princely—and their role was therefore passive at best. Again, Italian constitutions were urban, and jealously so. In Bologna, countryfolk were citizens, registered in the voters' Book of Paradise, and served in the militia. But they rarely came to town and were not encouraged to. The weight given the gilds, furthermore, assured control to the population's middle elements, ranging from well-off merchants to those who owned or operated a workshop or store. While militia societies and regional representation often gave the proletariat a voice, the constant struggle to form minor gilds included in government indicates that its sound was very weak.

The *Grandi,* the noble or the rich who lived nobly, were also often pushed aside by plebeian legislation. Late thirteenth century Italian constitutions often insisted upon gild membership, even defining it as work with the hands. On the other hand, except at moments of crisis, the *Grandi* were not as disenfranchised as this implies. Rigorous application of blue-nail laws would have resulted in the extinction of plebeian leadership itself. Moreover, the generous granting of knighthood during popular victories evinces the usual ambivalence of new men toward aristocracy. Equality was only a weapon for lesser men: they knew better than to believe it. Lastly, the aristocracy provided the usual deviants, those who found empire in the rise of popular parties. In 1292, a knight, Giano delle Bella, led the middle gilds to power in Florence.

Indeed, Giano's life poses the problem of office in

democratic society. Only wealthy or professional men could exercise office efficaciously. Even when offices were paid, the artisan bent on making a name in government lost out in his profession. As Charles Petit-Dutaillis has shown for France, moreover, he sometimes lost more than just his craft. Never having stopped to learn, he lacked competence in his new role, and therefore lost his wits as well. Usually, however, the progeny of new men studied law and thus entered the political hierarchy. Although responsive to popular pressure, it is patent that their interest was not that of their fathers.

Reservations aside, however, the thirteenth century's end witnessed the highest achievement of Italian democracy in the medieval period. This peak was represented in grand political theory. The great polemicist Marsiglio of Padua expressed its politically moderate and stable ambitions in a style that sounded for centuries. (*See Documents Nos. 15, 16.*) Echoing the emperor Frederick II, the French monarchist Peter Dubois cursed the Lombards for it. The moderate monarchist, Giles of Rome, perceived that in Italy "the many as the whole people commonly ruled," and believed that, so long as this government aided each social order to its due achievement, it was right and beneficial.

It was precisely this fulfillment, however, that the Italian town failed to attain. Translation of power from the few to the many was not accompanied by wider harmony. Such is man's nature that each group strives to impose its view of the ideal state upon the others. Aristocracy fought to retain mastery, and lesser elements to expropriate the rich. Government became the arena of social war. In 1292 alone, Florence expropriated and exiled no less than seventy-three families, the lesser half of the landed and urban aristocracy. This vehemence was partly due to the medieval tradition of urban revolution. In times past, republicanism had won by revolt against the old princely state. Each successive group that sought power inherited the memory of successful revolt. (*See Document No. 9E.*)

By the early fourteenth century, however, revolution no longer worked. Social groups were too well balanced. The many were weakened by individual powerlessness; the few by lack of numbers. The downward passage of political and social power had reached its final term. Instilled hope and economic crisis, however, made man play the game out to the bitter end. The Florentine carder Ciuto Brandini was executed in 1345 for plotting a workers' uprising. His artisans were to act alone, without summoning foreigners or military adventurers. This was wisdom: with artisan aid three years before, Walter of Brienne almost established a French tyranny. In earlier and happier times, temporary dictatorships had often implemented the rise to power of lesser social groups. By now, however, tyrants were invited to come and serve, but remained to rule. Further, Brandini wanted no alignment with the *Grandi* or the rich against his enemies of the middle gilds. This was not wisdom. It was revolutionary preciosity: workers alone could not defeat the whole community.

Social disorder made mockery of republican institutions. An election became occasion for rebellion. From Dante's time, most great intellects sought ways to peace and looked to monarchy to end party strife. (*See Document No. 17.*) More, the relatively democratic age of Italian republicanism laid the foundations for the later principate. In the age of social struggle, each party in office sought to assure a broad and lengthy application of its political doctrines. This required emergency powers and extraordinary offices. Office terms lengthened, and investigatory rights were multiplied. Old constitutions were insufficient to express the expanded functions of the new state. Sometimes, traditional offices expanded to meet new needs. This was not usual, however. The *potestas,* for example, had been so early limited by aristocratic fear of princely power that it rarely developed into extraordinary magistracy. On the other hand, Captains of the People and other new offices created by the rise of popular parties were less inhibited. (*See Documents Nos. 9D, 40.*)

Temporary dictatorships or special magistracies were usually proposed by popular parties and approved by Public Parliaments. The people had less time for public business than the aristocracies and therefore relied more upon executive authority granted their electees. On the other hand, many extraordinary powers originated to defend the status of the well-to-do and aristocratic. In its very origin, then, extraordinary magistracy lacked firm commitment to social groups or parties. In this, it presaged the later principate.

The new officer or commission of officers entrusted with extraordinary functions was usually granted *liberum arbitrium,* or free will, within a certain sphere. When the officer was elected for a long term or lifetime, this grant gave him an almost princely prerogative. (*See Document No. 39.*) Once in power, the officer's interest was not to be solely dependent upon those who elected him. In one way, his consequent leaning toward old enemies fulfilled society's need for peace and exhibited the capacity to arbitrate that marks the true prince. In another way, however, it was the fulfillment of party passion. Temporary dictators often abolished all parties save those which supported themselves. This was a continuation of the earlier party design to cement itself in power. Party totalitarianism had led to the establishment of the prince and his party. (*See Documents Nos. 9G, 18, 46D and E.*)

The Prince. But we do not have real princes here. The abstraction of the estate princely from society's other estates could come about only when succession was vested in a family line. Early in the development of extraordinary magistracy, however, officers were empowered to use the state's resources for the protection of their families from retribution. The most secure protection was succession to office. It took generations to define this. Family succession was at first assured by election and association in office during the life of the incumbent. Even when hereditary right was established, families were still dominated by private law traditions. Inheritances were divided up, weakening the state and opening the door to party conflict. It was only in the fifteenth century that primogeniture was generalized in Italy. Milan, the most precocious princely state, achieved this in 1396.

Authentication of the prince's public authority was a matter of concern throughout this period. Rigorists lamented that Italy was ruled by tyrants, those who gained command by suasion and unconstitutional means. Humanists and jurists vied to condemn or adulate princes. (*See Documents Nos. 18-20.*) Legally, the rigorists were right. The extraordinary magistracy that prepared the way for princely power was alone such an innovation as to be unconstitutional. But this is not surprising. The old

republican constitutions had themselves been born in
revolt and tumult. The new principate merely continued
an old tradition.

The exercise of office *gratia populi* is, however, an
inelegant and deficient constitutional base for princely
power. It does not describe an estate above all other
estates. Princely free will was best expressed by the
plenitude of power *gratia dei*. The source of such power
traditionally lay in the empire. By 1396, the Visconti of
Milan gained hereditary right to the office of imperial
vicar. Perhaps this final need for princely authentication
was one reason, although minor, for the invasion of Italy
by the empire, France, and Spain in the late fifteenth century.

Not every northern and central Italian town underwent
the same evolution or experienced it in the same way.
There is today one medieval republic, San Marino. Moreover, progress was fast in some towns and slow in others.
While Milan led the way to princely power, Florence
fought hard against it. The covert principate of the Medici
was finally enthroned by pope and emperor only upon
the extinction of the Savonarolan movements in 1531.
And this resistance left behind memorials that inspired the
republicanism of later ages. Again, a transmuted form
of aristocratic republicanism sometimes managed to retain power. The rise of the first extraordinary magistracies
and dictatorships in the late thirteenth and fourteenth
centuries provoked a general reaction. Before the Medici
acquired seignory with popular backing in 1434, a
limited electorate froze into power and ruled by the
peculiar expedient of secret councils. Much the same was
true of Siena before 1487. Only the maritime republics of
Venice and, to a lesser extent, Genoa really developed this
system. From 1296, Venice built a collective monarchy
ruled by a narrow and hereditary elite of administrators
and warriors. The long stability of this curious constitution is practically unique in the history of the western
state.

In general, however, the principate triumphed. Naturally, parts of the old constitutions remained in force.
Much private business and law went on without direct
princely intervention. The prince specialized in the maintenance of peace and community defense. On the whole,

however, society evolved to augment effective princely
control. Ordered into gilds and economically protected by
them, the people at large were deprived of participation in
political life. Retaining wealth and mercantile interests,
aristocratic and wealthy elements were increasingly centered around the princely court. Nobility was granted as
reward for service. The political disenfranchisement of
the people was advantageous to the prince. It reduced
participation in the councils of government to an aristocracy of office that was separated from the mass and
viewed somewhat hostilely by it. The remnants of the
republican tradition had become aristocratic and un-
popular.

In the rest of Europe, basic political tendencies and
movements were the same, though later in time, sometimes
much later. Almost everywhere, the middle and lesser gilds
rose and sought to exercise power. Occasionally, partial
analogues to Italian extraordinary or princely magistracies
are seen. As Captain-general, the tribune Jacob of Arte-
velde ruled Ghent from 1337 to 1345. At Zürich in 1336,
an era of social trouble resulted in the lifetime dictatorship
of the mayor. In short, northern urbanism evolved in
the same direction as that of the Mediterranean. (*See
Documents Nos. 12, 13.*)

On the other hand, the northern town underwent its
development in a very different context. There was
generally no need to create monarchy; it was already
there. In France, for example, the analogue to the
growing Italian principate was the development of royal
power at the expense of liberties and self-government
attained by the towns in the past. The cause was similar
also: social conflicts between popular and aristocratic
elements invited arbitration. As usual, the royal state was
opportunist. At Sens in 1320, the king intervened to protect the poor upon their invitation. (*See Document No.
41.*) At Amiens in 1383, the reverse was true. The
monarchy's impartiality is shown by its fiscal policies.
Lesser social elements wanted a graduated tax on real
property and income—the famous *estime*. Patricians tried
either to corrupt this to their own advantage or to base
revenue upon market tolls and taxes. Regulating this
dispute, royal officers were happy to collect both. (*See
Document No. 12.*)

A further difference was that the unit of political power was larger in the north than in the south, in the western Mediterranean than in the center. Much of the battling over town rights, therefore, went on outside the town in provincial or national estates or parliaments. The history of the estates movement is not pertinent here, although it may be useful to remind ourselves that town representatives played no more of a role than the other orders in these assemblies in their attempt to control royal power. For our present purpose, the estates movement recalls the significance of provincial and national unification in mobilizing late medieval society. (*See Documents Nos. 45, 46.*)

Law and Justice. The diminution of local autonomy and the rise of the prince everywhere characterized urban life. Along with this evolution went profound changes in conceptions of law and social organization. Informed by Roman law, late medieval town law was more majestic than the rudimentary systems of the earlier day. To act, the judge no longer awaited the appeal to intervene by a hurt party. The active sense of social justice that motivated him inspired the use of denunciation and the investigatory mechanism of the inquisition to seek out wrongdoing. Crime against society or its visible symbol, the prince, inspired the jurists to unparalleled rigors. Torture was employed not so much for information as for penitence: the criminal must confess and know his heinousness. Such was the subtle, wise, and terrifying law of the Old Regime, down to the eighteenth century.

The origins of this legal system are worth examining. Twelfth century law was dominated by aristocratic suspicion of princely might and the state. Free arbitration was the usual method of settling civil disputes. Necessarily, however, criminal and important civil cases came before state courts. But their authority was severely circumscribed. Exceptions aside, criminal actions were initiated by private accusation, *clamor*. Moreover, princely judicial authority was usually aided or exercised by elected assessors who played the role of arbitral judges. Lastly, jealous custom limited the prince's prerogative by regulating types of evidence and punishment. The consuls of Toulouse, for example, all but abolished the prosecution of adultery by insisting on evidence that none could hope to get. This was not because the consuls loved lovers, but simply because they did not love the prince. In short, judicial liberty derived from the tension between princely and aristocratic authority.

Two factors, however, combined to dissolve the system described above. The first was the weakening of the prince. Aristocratic suspicion of the state had less reason for being: the guard was dropped. The second factor was the amplification of the idea of the *universitas* as popular elements played an increasing role in making public policy. This idea made the state court the true representative of the people's electoral power. During the thirteenth century, therefore, a decline in free arbitration was noticeable. Moreover, the obstruction of state authority by the old system of assessors was no longer desirable. The judge or board of judges, directly elected or appointed by elected bodies, represented a state that no citizen could deny. In a sense, of course, this was a fiction because such judicial bodies really represented only those elements or parties momentarily dominant. For this reason, litigants required protection. Under the influence of Bolognese Roman law, therefore, the old assessor-judges either disappeared or evolved into something like the modern lawyer. The advocate protected his client by arguing from abstract equity as found in Roman law, a text above party and society. Here is the start of a more mature and sensitive conception of law than had hitherto prevailed in the medieval period.

On the other hand, the new law had terrors. Because it represented the *universitas*, nothing was allowed to stand in its way. The introduction of the new law witnessed the generalization of judicial torture and of the procedures of denunciation and inquisition. Also, its social sensitivity made the law totalitarian. Sports were sometimes forbidden because they inspired party rixation. Likelihood became a sufficient basis for starting investigation and sometimes a wide consensus expressed in terms of manifest and notorious crime was even enough to condemn a man. That this system of justice could be used for purposes of social war is evident. During the struggle between the popular parties and the *Grandi* in Italy, magistrates were given free will (*liberum arbitrium*) to increase but not to diminish punishments meted out to *Grandi*. Others were to be tortured without hurt of body, but not the *Grandi*. These were sometimes condemned by open presumption, "as if the case had been fully proved." (*See Documents Nos. 48B, C.*) In short, the law which the Italian prince enforced had come to him from the era of relatively democratic republicanism.

Social Estates. Another characteristic of the late middle ages was the division of society into estates. The typical division was the clergy, nobility, and commons. This latter estate was commonly subdivided into a political part, the *bourgeoisie,* and the usually non-political peasantry and town commonalty. These estates developed from earlier medieval orders in turn derived from those of late Rome. Emphasis was upon function and service, and remuneration by privilege and rights. In town and out, for example, the knightly military function always remained important and was passed on to the later nobility. But the reality behind these terms changed considerably during the middle ages.

By the twelfth century, the warrior function no longer sufficed to define knightly aristocracy. As society became richer and more articulated, other groups developed a tradition and tactic of war. Moreover, the principal aristocratic interest was to limit the service it owed the prince. As we have seen, that was achieved by gaining hereditary right to office and privilege. Moreover, hereditary right implies family, and family the lineage conceptions that fortified the knights in their exclusiveness. By emphasizing privilege and diminishing service, family right abolished the prince's minister or servile knight. While implementing the rise of aristocracies against princes, this had its unpleasant aspects. Service knighthood had been a way for lesser social elements to rise in the past.

The late middle ages witnessed a drastic change. In the Rhine-Loire region, for example, the knightly aristocracy was seriously invaded from below during the thirteenth century. Patrician burghers bought seignories and acquired titles. The problem was still broader. By the latter part of that century, town patriciates were also under attack from below. With the economic crisis of the next century, all aristocracy was jeopardized. The conception of lineage and family community began to break down under the attack of individualist principles enunciated in Roman law and implemented by the rise of lesser social elements that, as the jurists said, "had no lineage." In this context, aristocracy no longer fought the prince or state so much as it concentrated upon drawing the line below. It therefore fostered the privileges and exemptions that marked the status of the late medieval and early modern nobility.

Having the general right, the state was summoned to protect the nobility by making it into a privileged order to which public authority controlled access. The price for this service was high, however, and a prince, such as the king of France, derived great profit from his defense of aristocratic status. Indeed from Italy's democratic republics to princely courts, the old conception of service and remunerative privilege was everywhere being renewed. Polemicists filled pages insisting that virtue—that difficult term!—and not heredity was nobility's true source. Princes and kings made use of the weakening of the hereditary principle. Aristocratic resistance was broken by the revived conception of service nobility.

What this meant for the history of urbanism is clear. As we have seen, the nobility traditionally lived in town in the Mediterranean. This was not typical in the north. During the later middle ages, however, it became more common. Service at the princely court brought the nobility to town. Further, ennoblement as the reward for service created an urban nobility. Of course this did not happen overnight. Even mature France distinguished the relatively urban nobility of the robe from the largely rural nobility of the sword. In northern Germany, it was only in the seventeenth century that the nobility began to live in town. In general, however, the mobilization of provinces and nations together with the conception of service nobility gradually brought town and countryside together and made the northern town more like its Mediterranean counterpart.

In the meantime, the lower orders of town society developed noticeably. With the exception of towns that boasted hereditary knightly orders, twelfth century town law knew only citizens or burghers. With the rise of popular parties and the maturing of town society, however, the old system went by the board. Its implication of equality or identity became too inaccurate for jurists and thinkers. A more elaborate social vocabulary developed and found its way into law. Florentine chroniclers distinguished between the *Grandi,* the *popolo grasso, medio,* and *minuto.* More significant was the split between the burghers and commonalty. In southern France, for example, edicts were addressed to burghers *and* commonalty or *menestrals. Menestrals* meant artisans or shopkeepers, those who exercised a ministry or profession with their hands. A thirteenth century Catalan jurist explained the distinction by defining the burgher as one who exercised a craft or profession but not with his hands. During the rise of popular elements, then, a perceptive legal system increasingly differentiated between social groups. Jurists worked to make the forms of judicial procedure and punishment reflect the actualities of social distinctions.

The prince inherited and developed these distinctions. For the political reasons examined earlier in this chapter, the artisans and shopkeepers were built into an order whose functions and privileges were primarily economic. Entrepreneurial and professional, the burghers remained a political order acting as representatives in the provincial or national estates and as recruits for princely offices. A system of social and functional groups had been rebuilt, and it therefore comes as no surprise that late Rome's law became Europe's textbook in the early modern period. It is also worth emphasizing again that in Italy, for example, the foundations of this social jurisprudence had been laid in the era of relatively democratic republicanism.

Prince and Burgher. These remarks about function remind us that the princely state had a particularly close relationship to the town. The state was centralist, and the town function of communication served centralization. Moreover, the town accumulated fluid capital in reservoirs that could be easily and conveniently tapped for state needs. Lastly, burghers were the favored recruits—along with certain lesser noble elements—for administrative and civil offices. The reason for this was twofold. First, town populations were relatively more literate than rural. The second reason is more complex.

As Montesquieu pointed out, the main limitation of princely power comes from those to whom custom accords imprescriptible rights and privileges. The principal group of this kind was the nobility. The grant of hereditary privilege in return for state service represents the degree to which society resisted the imposition of total controls by the monarch in the late middle ages. Enlightened princes of later times, therefore, tried to abolish irrational privilege, making all men equal in service to the state. In the earlier period, however, the issues were not yet this clear, and Italian princes and French kings were satisfied to recruit the relatively unprivileged burghers for their service. They were mostly the prince's men; the nobles were largely their own. This is important because it reminds us that townsmen were not the masters. The monarch was the one who ruled. In 1463, Louis XI asserted his right to change any town constitution at his good pleasure and will "without anyone doing more than watching."

Our survey of western town life has brought us into the fifteenth century, the start of the modern era. The first years of that century were not happy for Italy, France, and adjacent regions, Europe's heartland. Sickness, social trouble, war, and impoverishment weighed man down. The future, however, was to be brighter. True, our evidence forbids us to speak of a vast accumulation of wealth opening the way to a new world. The year 1400 compares but poorly with 1300. But we also see that the time of troubles had stimulated and not disrupted Europe's power. New agencies had been created, capable of concentrating unprecedented amounts of human energy and wealth for specific purposes. New specializations implemented the mobilization of larger resources and bigger areas. European man had been ranked into social and economic units that limited particular rights for the benefit of common purposes.

The restrictive aspects of this corporatism are obvious. They were minimized, however, by the appearance and activities of as astonishing a group of individuals as history records. What a Jacques Coeur was to finance, a Valla was to the intellect, a Gonsalvo of Cordova to the battlefield. Corporate society constantly produced its opposite: the heroic individual. That the grandeur, violence, and license that marked the great had but one source is shown by the fact that they were all courtiers of princes

and kings. Above and apart from all other estates whose
functions were service, the estate princely both symbol-
ized and subsumed man's image of liberty. (*See Documents Nos. 17, 19, 41.*) "For such is our pleasure," wrote
Louis XI, "and, if it be done otherwise, we will not be
content in you."

— 8 —

CONCLUSION

The modern historian of town life is the heir of the
bourgeois thinkers of nineteenth century Europe. Lively
and fascinating polemicists that they were, these forefathers of our historical thought believed that they found
the source and the justification of their revolutions and of
the liberty that they stole from their princes in the histories of their towns. They taught us to freight the town
in history with an ideological baggage that it has no call to
carry. Again, living as we do in the throes of a technological revolution that has had no parallel in human history since late neolithic times, the immense city is everywhere about us. So oppressive, so weighty is this city that
we can hardly help but feel that it is itself alive and that
it evolves in ways which it determines without our puny
help. Our teachers and our experience, therefore, conspire to make us exaggerate the meaning of urbanism.

To discuss only one part of this problem, it is often
argued that the town possesses a necessary and characteristic ideology. Secularism, for example, or the Renaissance
spirit are said to be essentially urban in character. True
enough, towns attacked clerical privilege in the later middle ages. In 1239, Eichstadt expelled the clergy and
elected its own, a startling anticipation of the later Swiss
Reform. Padua fought Rome to a concordat as early as

1290. On the other hand, we do well to remember that Toulouse witnessed the first terrors of the Inquisition and that the Florentines listened avidly to the most famous Franciscan and Dominican orators. Again, it is certain that, with the growth of a lay legal profession, the town preceded the countryside in building the institutional base for the secular ethics and philosophy associated with the Renaissance and the Reformation. But the town *per se* was not secularist. In the earlier age . . . what need we say? Papal Rome was a city, and the most renowned scholastics taught at Paris, by far the largest town in northern Europe. As we have already seen, also, the same point may be made about politics. Like that of antiquity, the medieval town had no one characteristic form of polity. When not monarchical, the town was republican. But either the few or the many ruled the republic. Moreover, monarchy was perfectly at home in town. The Louvre was in Paris, and the Valois was never so replete with majesty as when he entered his capital.

Naturally, we do not contend that townsmen did not have ideas that were often distinct from those of the rest of society. Our analysis of medieval town life has demonstrated that the conflicting interests of town and countryside were reflected in the clash of ideas. When the western town first became Christian, we recall, the village remained doggedly pagan. What we must also remember, however, is that this evidence does not entitle us to distinguish between urban and rural men in any absolute way. Their differences reflected the transitory fact of the historical moment. But how much more significant were their basic similarities. In fact, urban history teaches us that town life has no ideology of any kind peculiar to itself.

The history of the town, however, has more positive uses than simply correcting mistaken notions about the past. It lends perspective to our historical thought. Like church history, it obliges us to go behind our immediate origins and to look back toward the source of our civilization, to the Mediterranean. There, we find the beginnings of a movement, a movement of countless millions of men lasting for upwards of five thousand years. Often interrupted, counter-attacked, and altered by local circumstance, this movement is that of an urban civilization that progressed from the eastern Mediterranean to Europe, and from Europe to the world.

Each age in this long history has its own unique interest and message. Along the shores of the Mediterranean in the middle ages, for example, we perceive a society generally more mature—that is to say, more populous, more complex, more urbanized—than that of northern Europe. Comparison of the Mediterranean with northern regions shows that the experience of man in mature society is more complete and more extreme, though perhaps less happy, than that of those who inhabit barely settled peripheries or open frontiers. As an instance of this, we may compare the political experience of the Lombard town-dweller with his counterpart in northern Europe. During the middle ages, the Lombards' journey led them from Roman monarchy to aristocratic republic, even to democracy, and back again to princely government. The burghers of northern Europe followed the same general course. But in the north, none of these types of government ever developed in quite as clear-cut a form as it did in Italy. Dealing with northern Europe alone, an unwary historian might almost speak only of monarchy.

These perspectives can aid us to prepare for our lives. Like other peoples, we Americans often use history as though it were a shallow mirror, to look in it only for ourselves, our present institutions, and our immediate origins. Our history becomes a sort of genealogical chronicle, touched up by iconodules and occasionally defaced by iconoclasts. Our voyage in history is hastily conceived and self-centered. Leaving antique Rome, we spend our middle ages in England, and our modern times in America. Our history is forever colonial, always a record of the province just beginning to be filled up. Our annals, in short, leave us as innocent as we were before we read them. We are pure, perhaps, but we are pitifully unprepared for adulthood. Surely, it is now time that our history prepare us for life in mature society.

Part Two

DOCUMENTS

The following translations have been chosen to document the principal assertions of the historical essay. They range in time across five centuries; in geography over all Europe. At least a third of the documents appear for the first time in English. Most, if not all, find their introduction in the text.

Yet some limitations remain and need be explained. Although a good deal necessarily has been said in Part One of the decline of Rome, we have not felt it necessary to include any documents from this period. Translations of classical and late-classical works are legion; the reader especially interested in ancient social and political ideas is referred to Ernest Barker's recent *From Alexander to Constantine*.

For a different reason we do little with the period 400-1100: poverty of the sources. Every historian of municipal origins has produced his own theory because each deals with more or less the same few and fragmentary survivals of written or archeological evidence and brings to their interpretation a peculiar slant based upon his national prejudice or a new scrap or two of evidence. To have ranged here a list of three- or four-line passages dating from the ninth or tenth centuries would have been meaningless and confusing.

Throughout the essay emphasis has been placed upon Mediterranean, especially Italian, activities; yet the reader will find in the document section a good number of translations from English sources. We have given this emphasis because of the excellence of some recent translations; because of the intrinsic as well as representative importance of some of the English documents; and also because of the greater comprehensibility of English evidence to an audience presumably unfamiliar with the details of continental medieval history.

I DESCRIPTIONS OF TOWNS

— Document No. 1 —

MOSLEM TOWNS IN NORTH AFRICA, ca. 977 A.D. [3]

Kairouan, the largest town of the Maghrib, surpasses all others in its commerce, its riches, and the beauty of its buildings and bazars. It is the seat of government of the whole Maghrib, the center to which flows the wealth of the land, and the residence of the sultan of that country. I heard from Abu al-Hasan . . . head of the (public) treasury in A.H. 336 (A.D. 947-48), that the income of all provinces and localities of the Maghrib . . . was between seven hundred and eight hundred million dinars. . . .

The exports from the Maghrib to the East are fair mulatto girls, who become concubines of the Abbasid princes and of other (great persons); many sultans were born of these women. . . . Other exports are young and handsome European slaves, amber, silks, suits of very fine woolen, fineries, woolen skirts, carpets, iron lead mercury, eunuchs from the countries of the Negroes and of the Slavs. People there possess excellent draft horses and camels innured to fatigue, which they procure from the Berbers. . . .

Kairouan and Sijilmasa are similar in salubrity of climate and in their nearness to the desert. Rich caravans

---

[3] From Abu-al-Qasim Muhammamed ibn Hawqal, *The Book of the Routes and the Kingdoms,* as quoted in R. S. Lopez, I. W. Raymond, *Medieval Trade in the Mediterranean World* (New York, 1955), pp. 52-4.

constantly leave Sijilmasa for the Sudan and bring great profits to the inhabitants of that town. . . . The inhabitants of other owns in that country (Maghrib) perhaps resemble those of Sijilmasa in their characteristics and the conditions of their existence, but they are inferior to the latter in wealth and comforts. . . .

— Document No. 2 —

AMALFI AND NAPLES, c. 977 [4]

The territory of Calabria borders on that of Lombardy, the first state of which is Salerno. Then there is Amalfi, the most prosperous town in Lombardy, the most noble, the most illustrious on account of its conditions, the most affluent and opulent. The territory of Amalfi borders on that of Naples. This is a fair city, but less important than Amalfi. The main wealth of Naples is linen and linen cloth. I have seen there pieces the like of which I found in no other country, and there is no craftsman in any other workshop in the world who is able to manufacture it. They are woven 100 *dhira* (in length) by 15 or 10 (in width), and they sell for 150 *ruba'i* a piece, more or less.

[4] *Ibid.,* p. 54.

— Document No. 3 —

THE CITY OF CONSTANTINOPLE, 1160-1163 [5]

The circumference of the city of Constantinople is eighteen miles. . . . Great stir and bustle prevails at Constantinople in consequence of the conflux of many merchants, who resort thither, by land and by sea, from all parts of the world for purposes of trade. In this respect the city is equalled only by Bagdad, the metropolis of the Mohammedans. At Constantinople is the place of worship called St. Sophia, and the metropolitan seat of the pope of the Greeks, who are at variance with the pope of Rome. It contains as many altars as there are days of the year, and possesses innumerable riches, which are augmented every year by the contributions of the two islands and of the adjacent towns and villages. All the other places of worship in the whole world do not equal St. Sophia in riches. . . . The Hippodrome is a public place near the wall of the palace, set aside for the king's sports. Every year the birthday of Jesus the Nazarene is celebrated there with public rejoicings. On these occasions you may see there representations of all the nations who inhabit the different parts of the world, with surprising feats of jugglery. . . .

The tribute which is brought to Constantinople every year from all parts of Greece, consisting of silks and purple cloths and gold, fills many towers. These riches and buildings are equalled nowhere in the world. . . . The number of Jews at Constantinople amounts to two thousand Rabbanites and five hundred Caraites, who live in

[5] From Benjamin of Tudela in Thomas Wright, *Early Travels in Palestine* (London, 1848), as quoted in G. G. Coulton, *Social Life in Britain from the Conquest to the Reformation* (Cambridge, 1919), pp. 412-13. Abridged.

one spot, but divided by a wall. . . . Many of them are manufacturers of silk cloths, many others are merchants, some being extremely rich; but no Jew is allowed to ride upon a horse except R. Solomon Hamitsri, who is the king's physician, and by whose influence the Jews enjoy many advantages even in their state of oppression, which is very severely felt by them. . . . The quarter inhabited by the Jews is called Pera.

— Document No. 4 —

DESCRIPTION OF MILAN, 1288 [6]

In regard to housing . . . the truth is there before the eyes of those who see. The streets in this city are quite wide, the palaces quite beautiful, the houses packed in, not scattered but continuous, stately, adorned in a stately manner.

1. Dwellings with doors giving access to the public streets have been found to number about 12,500, and in their number are very many in which many families live together with crowds of dependents. And this indicates the astonishing density of population of citizens.

2. The roofed commons (open to all) neighbors in those squares which are popularly called *coperti* almost reach the record number of sixty.

3. The court of the Commune, befitting such a great city, spreads over an area of two *pertiche* or thereabouts. And in order to make this more understandable perchance

[6] Bonvicinus de Rippa, *De magnalibus urbis Mediolani*, ed. F. Novati in *Bollettino dell'Istituto Storico Italiano*, XX (1898), pp. 67-114, as quoted in Lopez and Raymond, *Medieval Trade in the Mediterranean World* (New York, 1955), pp. 61 ff.

to some people, (I shall specify that it) measures 130 cubits from east to west and 136 from north to south. In the midst of it stands a wonderful palace and in the court itself there is a tower, in which are the four bells of the Commune. On the eastern side is a palace in which are the rooms of the podestà, and of the judges, and at its end on the northern side is the chapel of the podestà, built in honor of our patron, the Blessed Ambrose. And another palace prolongs the court on the north; so, similarly, on the west. To the south there is also the hall where the sentences of condemnation are publicly proclaimed.

5. . . . Outside the wall of the moat there are so many suburban houses that they alone would be enough to constitute a city. . . .

6. The main gates of the city are also very strong, and they reach the number of six. The secondary gates, named *pusterle,* are ten. . . .

7. The sanctuaries of the saints . . . are about two hundred in the city alone, having 480 altars. . . .

9. The steeples, built in the manner of towers, are about 120 in the city. . . .

10. In the country there are pleasant and delightful localities, even stately towns, fifty in number; and among them is Monza, ten miles distant from the ctiy, worthier to be named a city than a town. Indeed, 150 villages with castles are subject to the jurisdiction of our Commune, and among them there are a great many, each of which has more than five hundred inhabitants able to bear arms. And in these very towns as well as in the villages not only farmers and craftsmen live but also many magnates of high nobility. And there also are other isolated buildings, some of which are called mills, and others, popularly, *cassine*—the infinite number of which I can hardly estimate. . . .

— Document No. 5 —

WILLIAM FITZ STEPHEN'S DESCRIPTION OF LONDON, 1170-1183[7]

Among the noble and celebrated cities of the world that of London, the capital of the kingdom of the English, is one which extends its glory farther than all the others and sends its wealth and merchandise more widely into distant lands. Higher than all the rest does it lift its head. It is happy in the healthiness of its air; in its observance of Christian practice; in the strength of its fortifications; in its natural situation; in the honour of its citizens; and in the modesty of its matrons. It is cheerful in its sports, and the fruitful mother of noble men. Let us look into these things in turn.

In the church of St. Paul, there is the episcopal seat. Once it was metropolitan, and some think it will again become so, if the citizens return to the island, unless perhaps the archiepiscopal title of the blessed martyr, Thomas, and the presence of his body preserves that dignity for ever at Canterbury where it is at present. . . . As regards the practice of Christian worship, there are in London and its suburbs thirteen greater conventual churches, and besides these, one hundred and twenty-six lesser parish churches.

It has on the east side the Palatine castle, very great

[7] From *English Historical Documents, 1140-1189,* edited by D. C. Douglas and G. W. Greenway, 1953, pp. 956 ff. Reprinted by permission of Oxford University Press, Inc., New York.

and strong: the keep and walls rise from very deep foundations and are fixed with a mortar tempered by the blood of animals. On the west there are two castles very strongly fortified, and from these there runs a high and massive wall with seven double gates and with towers along the north at regular intervals. London was once also walled and turreted on the south, but the mighty Thames, so full of fish, has with the sea's ebb and flow washed against, loosened, and thrown down these walls in the course of time. . . .

Immediately outside of one of the gates there is a field which is smooth both in fact and in name. On every sixth day of the week, unless it be a major feastday, there takes place here a famous exhibition of fine horses for sale. . . .

By themselves in another part of the field stand the goods of the countryfolk: implements of husbandry, swine with long flanks, cows with full udders, oxen of immense size, and wooly sheep. There also stand the mares fit for plough, some big with foal, and others with brisk young colts following them closely.

To this city from every nation under heaven merchants delight to bring their trade by sea. The Arabian sends gold; the Sabaean spice and incense. The Scythian brings arms, and from the rich fat lands of Babylon comes oil of palms. The Nile sends precious stones; the men of Norway and Russia furs and sables; nor is China absent with purple silk. The Gauls come with their wines.

London, as historians have shown, is a much older city than Rome, for though it derives from the same Trojan ancestors, it was founded by Brutus before Rome was founded by Romulus and Remus. Wherefore they still have the same laws from the common origin. This city like Rome is divided into wards; it has annual sheriffs instead of consuls; it has its senatorial order and lower magistracies; it has drains and aqueducts in its streets; it has its appointed places for the hearing of cases deliberative, demonstrative, and judicial; it has its several courts, and its separate assemblies on appointed days.

II HISTORICAL ACCOUNTS

Section 1: Italy

— Document No. 6 —

LOMBARD SOCIETY IN THE MID-TWELFTH CENTURY [8]

Nevertheless the Lombards had laid aside all the bitterness of their barbarous ferocity, in consequence, perhaps, of their marriages with the Italians, so that they had children who inherited something of Roman mildness and intellect from their maternal parentage, or from the influence of the soil and climate, and retain the elegance of the Latin language and a certain courtesy of manners. They also imitate the activity of the ancient Romans in the management of cities and in the preservation of the state. Finally, they are so attached to their liberty that, to avoid the insolence of rulers, they prefer to be reigned over by consuls than by princes. And since, as it is known, there are three orders among them, of captains, vassals, and the commons, in order to keep down arrogance, these aforesaid consuls are chosen, not from one order, but from each, and, lest they should be seized with a greed for power, they are changed nearly every year. From which it happens that the territory is all divided into cities, which have each reduced those of their own prov-

---

[8] From Otto of Freising's *Gesta Frederici imperatoris,* as published in U. Balzani, *Early Chroniclers of Italy* (London, 1883), pp. 253-55. Otto of Freising (c. 1114-1158) was a German bishop and distinguished historian, closely related to the German imperial court.

ince to live with them, so that there is hardly to be found any noble or great man with so great an influence, as not to owe obedience to the rule of his own city. And they are all accustomed to call these various territories their own *Comitatus,* from this privilege of living together. And in order that the means of restraining their neighbors may not fail, they do not disdain to raise to the badge of knighthood, and to all grades of authority, young men of low condition, and even workmen of contemptible mechanical arts, such as other people drive away like the plague from the more honourable and liberal pursuits. From which it happens that they are pre-eminent among the other countries of the world for riches and power. And to this they are helped also, as has been said, by their own industrious habits and by the absence of their princes, accustomed to reside north of the Alps.

— Document No. 7 —

SOCIAL TROUBLES IN LOMBARDY, 1036[9]

At the same time, there was great trouble in Italy, the likes of which are unheard of in recent times. The trouble stemmed from the various sworn associations which the people made against their leaders. For, indeed, all the *valvassores* of Italy and the common soldiers swore against their lords, and all the lesser folk against the greater so that they prevented their lords from getting away with anything against their will. They said that if the emperor did not wish to appear on the scene in person, they would make the laws themselves. . . .

[9] From Wiponis Gesta Chuonradi Imperator, chap. 34, edited in H. Bresslau in *M.G.H. Scriptores rerum germanicarum in usum scholarum* (Hannover and Leipzig, 1915, 3rd. edition), p. 54.

— Document No. 8 —

SALIMBENE'S ACCOUNT OF THE THIRTEENTH CENTURY WARS IN ITALY, 1247[10]

When King Enzio[11] heard that the Guelf exiles had entered Parma by force, leaving the siege of Quinzano, he came by a forced night march, not singing but groaning inwardly, as is the wont of an army returning from a rout. I lived in those days in the convent of the Friars Minor at Cremona, wherefore I know all these things well. For at early dawn the men of Cremona were assembled forthwith with the King to a Council which lasted even to high tierce [i.e. past 9 o'clock]; after which they ate hurriedly and went forth to the very last man, with the *Carroccio* in their van.[12] There remained in Cremona not one man who was able to march and fight in battle; and I am fully persuaded that if they had marched without delay to Parma and quitted themselves like men, they would have recovered the city. For if one enemy knew how it fared in all things with his enemy, he might ofttimes smite him; but by the will of God King Enzio halted with the army of Cremona by the Taro Morto, and came not to Parma, that the Lord might not bring evil upon

---

[10] These excerpts are taken from G. G. Coulton, *From St. Francis to Dante* (London, 1906), pp. 55-56, 114-15, 217-18. Salimbene of Parma (1221-c. 1290) was a Franciscan and a chronicler.

[11] Enzio, King of Sardinia (c. 1220-1272), was a natural son of Frederick II, Emperor and King of Sicily and southern Italy.

[12] The *Carroccio* was the ornamented wagon or ark on which were placed the great banners of the town militia.

them. For he wished to wait there until his father should come from Turin. Meanwhile succor came daily from all parts to the men of Parma who had entered the city: and the citizens made themselves a ditch and a palisade, that their city might be shut in against the enemy. Then the Emperor, all inflamed with wrath and fury at that which had befallen him, came to Parma; and in the district called Grola, wherein is great plenty of vineyards and good wine (for the wine of that land is most excellent), he built a city, surrounded with great trenches, which also he called Victoria, as an omen of what should come to pass. . . .

1284

But here, that you may know the labyrinth of affairs, I must not omit to tell how the church party in Modena was driven forth from the city, while the Imperial party held it. So it was also in Reggio; and so also, in process of time, in Cremona. Therefore in those days was most cruel war, which endured many years. Men could neither plow, nor sow, nor reap, nor till vineyards, nor gather the vintage, nor dwell in the villages; more especially in the districts of Parma and Reggio and Modena and Cremona. Nevertheless, hard by the town walls, men tilled the fields under guard of the city militia, who were mustered quarter by quarter according to the number of the gates. Armed soldiers thus guarded the peasants at their work all day long; for so it must needs be, by reason of the ruffians and bandits and robbers who were multiplied beyond measure. For they would take men and lead them to their dungeons, to be ransomed for money; and the oxen they drove off to devour or sell. . . . And the land was made desert, so that there was neither husbandman nor wayfarer. . . .

So in this year 1284 the Pisans, seeing all the evil which the Genoese had inflicted upon them, and wishing to avenge themselves, built many ships and galleys and sea vessels, in the river Arno, and when the fleet had been made ready, they ordained that none betwixt the ages of 20 and 60 should stay at home, but that all should go to the fight. And they scoured the whole of the Genoese shore, destroying and burning, killing and taking captives, and plundering. And this they did all along the shore from

Genoa to Provence, desiring to find the Genoese and
fight with them. But the Genoese had ordained that
one of their citizens should remain at home between the
ages of 18 years and 70, for all must go to fight. Thus
they scoured the sea, desiring to find the Pisans. At least
they found each other between the point of Corsica and
Gorgona, and they grappled their ships together after
the fashion of sea-fights, and there they fought with such
slaughter on either side that even the heavens seemed
to weep in compassion, and many on either part were
slain, and many ships sunken. But when the Pisans had
already the upper hand, other Genoese came and fell
upon them, wearied as they were. Nevertheless the battle
still raged furiously on both sides. At last, the Pisans
finding themselves worsted, yielded themselves to the
Genoese who slew the wounded, and kept the rest in
prison: and even the victors who had no cause for boast-
ing, since fortune was cruel to either side, and there was
such weeping and wailing in Genoa and Pisa as was
never heard in those two cities from the day of their
foundation to our times.

— Document No. 9 —

SELECTIONS FROM VILLANI'S FLORENTINE HISTORY [13]

A. Book V, sec. 9 (1177): Florentine Social War

Wherefore in the self same year there began in Florence
dissension and great war among the citizens, the worst
that had ever been in Florence; and this was by reason of
too great prosperity and repose, together with pride and
ingratitude; forasmuch as the house of Uberti, which were
the most powerful and the greatest citizens of Florence,

[13] *Selections from the first nine books of the Croniche Fioren-
tine of Giovanni Villani,* translated by R. E. Selfe, ed. P. E.
Wicksteed (Westminister, 1897), pp. 109-110, 117-18, 140,
149-50, 225-28.

with their allies, both magnates and *popolani*,[14] began war against the Consuls (which were the lords and rulers of the commonwealth for a certain time and under certain ordinances), from envy of the Government, which was not to their mind; and the war was so fierce and unnatural that well-nigh every day, or every other day, the citizens fought against one another in divers parts of the city, from district to district, according as the factions were, and as they had fortified their towers, whereof there was great number in the city, in height 100 or 120 cubits. And in those times, by reason of the said war, many towers were newly fortified by the communities of the districts, from the common funds of the neighborhood, which were called Towers of the Fellowships, and upon them were set engines to shoot forth one at another, and the city was barricaded in many places; and this plague endured more than two years, and many died by reason thereof, and much peril and hurt was brought upon the city; but this war among the citizens became so much of use and wont that one day they would be fighting, and the next day they would be eating and drinking together, and telling tales of one another's valour and prowess in these battles; and at last they ceased fighting, in that it irked them for very weariness, and they made peace, and the Consuls remained in their government; albeit, in the end they begot and then brought forth the accursed factions, which were here afterwards in Florence, as hereafter in due time we will make mention.

B. BOOK V, SEC. 32 (1207): THE ELECTION OF THE FIRST PODESTA (POTESTAS)

In the year of Christ 1207, the Florentines chose for the first time a foreign magistrate, for until that time the city had been ruled by the government of citizen consuls, of the greatest and best of the city, with the council of the senate, to wit, 100 good men; and these consuls, after the manner of Rome, entirely guided and governed the city, and administered law and executed justice; and they remained in office for one year. And there were four consuls as long as the city was divided into quarters, one

[14] *Popolani* means plebs, those without titles. Magnates, or *magnati,* means knightly aristocracy, similar to the term *Grandi* used in the introductory essay.

to each gate; and afterwards there were six, when the city was divided into *sesti*. But our forefathers did not make mention of the names of all, but one of them of greatest estate and fame, saying, "In the time of such a consul and his colleagues"; but afterwards when the city was increased in inhabitants and in vices, and there came to be more ill-deeds, it was agreed for the good of the commonwealth, to the end the citizens might not have so great a burden of government, and that justice might not miscarry by reason of prayers, or fear, or private malice, or any other cause, that they should invite a gentleman from some other city who might be their Podestà for a year and administer civil justice with his assessors and judges, and carry into execution sentences and penalties on the person. And the first Podestà in Florence was Gualfredetto of Milan, in the said year; and he dwelt in the Bishop's Palace, forasmuch there was as yet no palace of the commonwealth in Florence. Yet the government of the consuls did not therefore cease, but they reserved to themselves the administration of all other things in the commonwealth. And by the said government the city was ruled until the time of the Primo Popolo in Florence, as hereafter we shall make mention, and then was created the office of the Ancients.

C. Book VI, sec. 26 (1237): Paving of the Streets of Florence

The year of Christ 1237, Messer Rubaconte da Mandella of Milan being Podestà of Florence, the new bridge was made in Florence, and he laid the first stone with his own hand, and threw the first trowelful of mortar, and from the name of the said Podestà the bridge was named Rubaconte. And during his government all the roads in Florence were paved; for before there was but little paving, save in certain particular places, master streets being paved with bricks; and through this convenience and work the city of Florence became more clean, and more beautiful, and more healthy.

D. Book VI, sec. 39 (1250): The Success of the *Primo Popolo*[15]

[15] *Primo popolo* refers to the first decisive success of the popular party.

When the said host came back to Florence there was great contention amongst the citizens, inasmuch as the Ghibellines,[16] who ruled the land, crushed the people with insupportable burdens, taxes, and imposts; and with little to show for it, for the Guelfs were already established up and down in the territory of Florence, holding many fortresses and making war upon the city. And besides all this, they of the house of the Uberti and all the other Ghibelline nobles tyrannized over the people with ruthless extortion and violence and outrage. Wherefore the good citizens of Florence, tumultuously gathering together, assembled themselves at the church of San Firenze; but not daring to remain there, because of the power of the Uberti, they went and took their stand at the church of the Minor Friars at Santa Croce, and remaining there under arms they dared not to return to their homes, lest when they had laid down their arms they should be broken by the Uberti and the other nobles and condemned by the magistrates. So they went under arms to the houses of the Anchioni of San Lorenzo, which were very strong, and there, still under arms, they forcibly elected thirty-six corporals of the people, and took away the rule from the Podestà, which was then in Florence, and removed all the officials. . . .

E. BOOK VII, SEC. 16 (1267): THE REORGANIZATION OF MUNICIPAL GOVERNMENT UPON THE EXPULSION OF THE GHIBELLINES

When the Guelf party had returned to Florence, and the vicar or Podestà was come from King Charles, and after twelve good men had been appointed, as of old, the Ancients, to rule the republic, the council of 100 good men of the people was restored, without whose deliberation no great thing or cost could be carried out; and after any measure had been passed in this council, it was put to the vote in the council of the colleges of consuls of the greater Arts, and the council of the credenza [privy council of the Captain of the People] of eighty. These councillors, which, when united with the

[16] The Ghibellines were imperialists and frequently noble. The Guelfs were pro-papal and frequently led popular parties. These original meanings were eventually confused, as the groups split up and developed into formal parties.

general council, numbered 300, were all *popolani* and
Guelfs. After measures had been passed in the said councils, the following day the same proposals were brought
before the councils of the Podestà, first before the council
of ninety, including both magnates and *popolani* (and with
them associated yet again the colleges of consuls of the
Arts), and then before the general council, which was of
300 men of every condition; and these were called the
occasional councils; and they had in their gift governor-
ships of fortresses, and dignities, and small and great
offices. And this ordered, they appointed revisors, and
corrected all statutes and ordinances, and ordered that
they should be issued each year. In this manner was
ordered the state and course of the commonwealth and of
the people of Florence at the return of the Guelfs; and
the chancellors of finance were the monks of Settimo and
of Ognissanti on alternate half-years.

F. BOOK VII, SEC. 17 (1267): THE ORGANIZATION OF THE
   GUELF PARTY

In these times, when the Ghibellines had been driven
out from Florence, the Guelfs which had returned thither
being at strife, concerning the goods of the Ghibelline
rebels, sent their ambassadors to the court, to Pope Urban
and to King Charles, to order their affairs, which Pope
Urban and King Charles for their estate and peace
ordered them in this manner, that the goods should be
divided into three parts—one part to be given to the
commonwealth, the second to be awarded in compensation to the Guelfs which had been ruined and exiled, the
third to be awarded for a certain time to the "Guelf
Party"; but afterwards all the said goods fell to the Party,
whence they formed a fund, and increased it every day,
as a reserve against the day of need of the Party; concerning which fund, when the Cardinal Ottaviano degli
Ubaldini heard thereof, he said, "Since the Guelfs of Florence have funded a reserve, the Ghibellines will never return thither." And by the command of the Pope and the
king, the said Guelfs made three knights heads of the
Party, and called them at first consuls of the knights, and
afterwards they called them Captains of the Party, and
they held office for two months, the *sesti* electing them
alternately, three and three; and they gathered to their

councils in the new church of Santa Maria Sopra Porta, being the most central place in the city, and where there are many Guelf houses around; and their privy council consisted of fourteen, and their larger council of seventy magnates and *popolani*, by whose vote were elected the Captains of the Party and other officers. And they called three magnates and three *popolani* Priors of the Party, to whom were committed the order and care of the money of the Party; and also one to hold the seal, and a syndic to prosecute the Ghibellines. And all their secret documents they deposited in the church of the Servi Sancte Marie. After like manner the Ghibelline refugees made ordinances and captains. We have said enough of the Ordinances of the Party, and we will return to the general events, and to other things.

Section 2: Northern Europe

— Document No. 10 —

THE COMMUNE AND PEACE ASSOCIATION OF LE MANS, 1070[17]

Since the city of Le Mans experienced many revolutions during the episcopacy of this bishop (Hoël), I think it not improper to recount in his biography the story of one of these revolutions a tale worthy of being remembered.

William, leader of the Normans, who had just annexed the county of Maine after the extinction and almost complete exhaustion of the heirs of this county, went with

[17] G. Busson and A. Ledru, edd. *Actus pontificum Cenomannis in urbe degentium* (Le Mans, 1901), pp. 376-79, published in Robert Latouche, *Textes d'histoire medievale* (Paris, 1951), pp. 236-39.

a great army of Frenchmen, Normans, men of Le Mans, and Bretons to England where he defeated the English in battle. Their king, Harold, having been killed, William conquered the entire kingdom of England. But while he stayed on in England on account of the war, the magnates of Maine, together with the people, ceased to be faithful and deserted him in great numbers. They sent a deputation to Italy to bring back a certain marquis, Atho by name, with his wife and his son Hughes, and they handed over both the city and the county to this marquis, chasing from the donjons and from the country itself all the Normans and the men of the king who lived in the city. They even massacred one of the king's officials named Onofredus whom they discovered in one of the donjons.

Seeing all this, the bishop hastened to flee from the city lest he give the impression of having aided the treason of the inhabitants, and having arrived in England after an easy crossing, he was received with great affection by the king. No sooner had his enemies learned this, than they took hold of his houses and all his possessions intending systematically to pillage everything that belonged to him. This is why the bishop after a short stay with the king took certain measures to regain his see with the king's permission; and the king gave him many presents. But since, because of their hate for the king of England, the citizens did not wish to let him re-enter the city at any price, he stayed with his entourage outside the city in the monastery of St. Vincent. However, his clerics who could not bear his absence concluded an agreement with his enemies and brought him back to his episcopal seat.

During this time the marquis Atho who had conquered the country by both force and generosity, discovered for himself the fickleness of the people of Le Mans. And when the money with which he had generously endowed them at the beginning began to disappear he discovered that their attitude of loyalty to him likewise began to disappear. At this point he returned to Italy, leaving his wife and his son in the hands of Geoffrey de Mayenne, a person of noble but crafty character. The wife of the marquis was named Gercende; she was the daughter of Herbert the illustrious count of Maine who had been nicknamed the "Watchdog." First married to Thibaut,

Duke of Champagne, she had been separated from him after a repudiation, and had then married the aforementioned Atho. Geoffrey, who had become her advisor and in effect her husband, sought every occasion to oppose the inhabitants and was forced to wipe out the new demands. In turn, they resolved to oppose his unjust actions and not to let themselves be unjustly oppressed either by him or anyone else.

Then having made an association which they called a commune, they joined themselves together by oaths, and forced the other magnates of the countryside to swear allegiance to their commune. Made bold by this conspiracy they began to commit innumerable crimes, condemning many people indiscriminately and without cause, blinding some for the smallest reasons and, horrible to say, hanging others for insignificant faults. They even burned the strongholds of the area during Lent, and what is worse during the period of the Passion of Our Lord. And all this they did without reason.

As one of the principal lords of the area, Hugh de Sille had, because of various violent acts, roused the passions of the confreres against him. These soon sent agents throughout the region rousing a great angry multitude against Hugh who opposed their association. Once assembled, this army threw itself with great enthusiasm against the castle of Sille, the bishop and the priests of the various churches leading the host with the cross and religious banners. While these people remained in the vicinity of the castle, Geoffrey of whom we have already spoken, quietly entered among them and pitched his camp nearby. And, having succeeded in making contact with the besieged through secret messengers, he worked in every way to obstruct the activities of the attackers. In the morning the besieged sallied forth from the castle and offered combat, but while our men, now awakened by the loud clamor of arms, prepared to fall on their enemies, a rumor started suddenly and swept through the camp. It had been spread by clever men who made known what was not in fact true, namely, that the city had been saved, and handed over to their enemies. The mob of peasants, terrified at the same time by the great noise and their enemies, threw down their arms and fled.

— Document No. 11 —

THE PEOPLE OF COLOGNE REBEL AGAINST THEIR ARCHBISHOP, 1074 [18]

The archbishop spent Easter in Cologne with his friend, the bishop of Münster, whom he had invited to celebrate this festival with him. When the bishop was ready to go home, the archbishop ordered his servants to get a suitable boat ready for him. They looked all about, and finally found a good boat which belonged to a rich merchant of the city, and demanded it for the archbishop's use. They ordered it to be got ready at once and threw out all the merchandise with which it was loaded. The merchant's servants, who had charge of the boat, resisted, but the archbishop's men threatened them with violence unless they immediately obeyed. The merchant's servants hastily ran to their lord and told him what had happened to the boat, and asked him what they should do. The merchant had a son who was both bold and strong. He was related to the great families of the city, and, because of his character, very popular. He hastily collected his servants and as many of the young men of the city as he could, rushed to the boat, ordered the servants of the archbishop to get out of it, and violently ejected them from it. The advocate of the city [19] was called in, but

---

[18] From Lambert of Hersfeld, Annals, *M.G.H. SS.* folio, V, p. 211 ff., as translated in O. J. Thatcher and E. H. McNeal, *A Source Book for Medieval History,* pp. 585-86. Copyright 1905 by Charles Scribner's Sons, 1933 by Oliver J. Thatcher. Reprinted with the permission of the publisher.

[19] The secular officer appointed to protect ecclesiastical property and rights.

116

his arrival only increased the tumult, and the merchant's son drove him off and put him to flight. The friends of both parties seized their arms and came to their aid, and it looked as if there were going to be a great battle fought in the city. The news of the struggle was carried to the archbishop, who immediately sent men to quell the riot, and being very angry, he threatened the rebellious young men with dire punishment in the next session of court. Now the archbishop was endowed with all virtues, and his uprightness in all matters, both of the state and of the church, had often been proved. But he had one vice. When he became angry, he could not control his tongue, but overwhelmed everybody, without distinction, with bitter upbraidings and violent vituperation. When his anger had passed, he regretted his fault and reproached himself for it. The riot in the city was finally quieted a little, but the young man, who was very angry as well as elated over his first success, kept on making all the disturbance he could. He went about the city making speeches to the people about the harsh government of the archbishop, and accused him of laying unjust burdens on the people, of depriving innocent persons of their property, and of insulting honorable citizens with his violent and offensive words. . . . It was not difficult for him to raise a mob. . . . Besides, they all regarded it as a great and glorious deed on the part of the people of Worms that they had driven out their bishop because he was governing them too rigidly.[20] And since they were more numerous and wealthy than the people of Worms, and had arms, they disliked to have it thought that they were not equal to the people of Worms in courage, and it seemed to them a disgrace to submit like women to the rule of the archbishop who was governing them in a tyrannical manner. . . .

[20] Worms had revolted in 1073.

— Document No. 12 —

THE RISING OF GHENT AGAINST THE PATRICIANS, 1301-1302 [21]

In the year of our Lord 1301, about the end of May, King Philip came into Flanders with the Queen of Navarre, his wife, as new prince and direct lord. . . . He came first to Douai, next to Lille, afterwards to Ghent. . . . Now when the king entered Ghent, the commonalty hastening to meet him, cried out loudly and begged earnestly to be freed from a certain heavy tax which there was at Ghent and Bruges upon articles for sale, especially beer and mead. The men of Ghent called it 'the evil money,' those of Bruges, the 'assize.' And the king, in cheerful mood and freshly arrived, acceded to the requests of those who clamored thus. This greatly displeased the patricians of the town, who were used to making profit from the said exaction, as at Bruges also. From Ghent the king went. . . to Bruges. The men of Bruges came to meet him with extravagant adornments of their garments, and with diverse joustings sent him presents of great value. Now the échevins[22] and patricians of Bruges had forbidden the commonalty on pain of death, to clamour to the king for the abolition of the assize, or make supplication to him, as had been done at Ghent. The commonalty, offended by this, stood on the king's arrival as though they were dumb, at which, it is said, the king was very much surprised. When the king had gone on to Wynendaele, a very beautiful residence of the former court, the échevins and patricians of Bruges, being desirous that the presents made to the king and the ornaments of the garments which

[21] From *Annals of Ghent,* ed. Hilda Johnstone (New York, 1951), pp. 12-14. Selections.

[22] *Échevins* is the French for *scabini,* for which see introductory essay.

118

they had prepared to wear when meeting him should be paid for out of the assize, and that the tunics and raiment of the commonalty should be paid for out of the commonalty's own resources, still further excited the commonalty to anger. Great disturbance and dissension therefore arose in the town. Its originator is said to have been a certain weaver called Peter, surnamed Coninck, and some of his adherents. So the bailiff, on the advice of the patricians and *échevins* of Bruges, seized him, together with about twenty-five leaders of the commonalty, and shut him up in the king's prison, formerly the court's, that is called the Steen. When the commonalty heard of this, stirred and provoked, they gathered together, forced those in charge of the prison to open it and brought out all their friends unharmed, both Peter and his followers. So their agitation calmed down for a while, though they were still suspicious of the ill-will of the patricians. . . .

1302

In the year of our Lord 1302, there began a painful and deadly war, long in incubation and incapable of appeasement, which came to birth at last with horrible and copious shedding of the blood of innumerable men. . . .

— Document No. 13 —

THE RISING OF BRISTOL AGAINST THE PRIVILEGES OF THE FOURTEEN, 1316[23]

Some time ago trouble arose in the town of Bristol over customs in seaport and market, privileges and other things, in which fourteen of the greater persons of this

[23] From the *Chronicles of the Reigns of Edward I and Edward II,* vol. II, p. 219, printed in C. W. Colby, *Selections from the Sources of English History* (New York, 1911), pp. 94-95.

town seemed to have a special right. The community resisted, stating that the burgesses were all of one condition and therefore equal as to liberties and privileges. Over matters of this sort frequent domestic quarrels arose, until in the king's court they asked for and received judges to examine the case and bring it to just conclusion. Forthwith the fourteen procured that outsiders should be associated in the inquiry. These, moreover, were believed to have been bribed and wholly brought over to the side of the fourteen. The community alleged that it would be contrary to the liberties of the town to try a local matter by the judgment of outsiders, but the judges held that such allegations were idle; so that in this respect they did not regard the liberties and privileges of the citizens. The leaders of the community, seeing that their exceptions were not admitted and their right was being taken from them by favour rather than by reason, left the hall, where according to custom the trial was going on, in a great state of agitation, and thus spoke to the commonalty: "Judges have come who favour our adversaries and admit outsiders to our prejudice, whereby we shall forever lose our rights." On these words the foolish crowd started a riot and the whole people was smitten with fear of a tumult. Forthwith returning with a large company they entered the hall where they proceeded to turn their right into outrage. With fists and sticks they began to assail the opposing party, and that day about twenty lives were suddenly and stupidly lost. Since a natural fear so attacked both gentle and simple that many jumped out of the windows from the top of the balcony, and in falling to the ground broke their legs or shins very badly. As for the judges, they feared for their lives and humbly sought leave to depart in peace. The mayor of the town after he had with the greatest difficulty calmed the fury of the mob, sent them away unharmed.

On account of this disturbance about eighty men were indicted, and after a careful inquiry held before the royal judges at Gloucester, were condemned. They were then demanded from the county, and not coming or obeying were declared to be exiles. But well fortified they remained within their town nor would obey the royal mandate unless it were carried out by force. . . .

III POLITICAL THEORY

— Document No. 14 —

EXCERPTS FROM JOHN OF VITERBO'S *BOOK ON THE GOVERNMENT OF CITIES*, c. 1228 [24]

A. On the Definition of Law and Justice

The definitions of Law and Justice need not be discussed here since they are amply treated in the Digest and the Institutes under the title "On Justice and Laws" [25]; nevertheless I am concerned in this treatise with Justice in another way. . . . Omitting, then, the problem of the origin and definition of Law, let us discuss podestas, leaders and administrative officials of the city, for there would be few laws in the city were there not men to whom the laws are given for safekeeping.

B. On the Protection of Churches, Hospitals, and Other Dedicated Places

Churches, hospitals, chapels and other venerated places are to be protected by the rulers, podestas and rectors of the city; and, indeed, all other such dedicated spots are to be cared for. The care of sacred things is a worthy

---

[24] From *"Iohannis Viterbiensis Liber de regimine civitatum,"* ed. by G. Salvemini in *Bibliotheca iuridica medii aevi* (Bologna, 1901), vol. III, pp. 220, 233, 246, 260. John of Viterbo was probably the same as John Boccazii who was *potestas* of Florence in 1228.

[25] This refers to Justinian's *Corpus Iuris Civilis*: *D.* 1.1 and *Inst.* 1.1.

offering to all-powerful God, and especially since we seek assistance in such places. Their rights, then, must be especially protected, and in these matters imperial laws shall not scorn the imitation of sacred canons or sacred and divine laws.

C. ON THE CARE OF WIDOWS AND ORPHANS

The podestà shall care then for the widow and the orphan, but although this injunction is stated in this manner . . . it should not be interpreted to imply that he should favor them in his legal judgments or in court, for the judge or podesta should show equal justice to all. . . . Rather these words, "You shall be the guardian of the widow and the orphan" should be interpreted to mean that he shall protect them from the oppression and slander of the stronger members of society. So, therefore, the orphans and widows and the other weaker members of the community are to have their rights maintained. . . .

D. ON THE PODESTA'S INSTALLATION

At the time that, or on the day that the podestà is to enter his office and assume his responsibilities, he shall hear mass and then, with the blessing of the Lord, enter the palace of the commune and take the throne of glory. He shall publish the laws and make certain that they are accepted and understood without contradiction. He shall have the new laws sent about and posted, and shall see to it that they are well composed and beneficial and satisfactory both to himself and to the city he leads; and he shall have them read at the first public assembly. . . . This general assembly shall be held on the first feast day of his reign, either the first Sunday or other holy day. . . . And after these laws have been read, he shall rise and end the assembly; nor shall he allow any citizen to rise to speak in this parliament, especially if there is contemporary strife within the city. But if a citizen does speak there, and if one from the other faction wishes to speak, the podestà shall allow him to do so. Otherwise justice would not be served on this occasion, which would be untoward and hateful. For justice must be done to all citizens.

In truth, there are certain cities in which this sort of assembly is not held at the beginning of the podesta's rule;

but rather the laws are proposed and read in a general council, as in the noble city of Florence. . . .

E. On Consultation with Councils and Parliaments

On those matters which are grave and serious and which touch the best interests of the city the podestà shall, the council of the city having been assembled, confer with the council, and shall do so again and again should the gravity of the situation so demand. "But in the multitude of counsellors there is safety" (Proverbs XI, 14). Then, certain, the podesta may act with the knowledge and advice of the city's council. . . . But if the importance of the crisis demands yet greater counsel, other of the wiser citizens elected by the entire citizenry should be summoned to give it; that is, representatives of the judges and lawyers, consuls of the merchants and bankers, priors of the guilds; and also representatives of all others knowledgeable with regard to the issue. These shall be summoned so that the gravity of the situation may be known to all in positions of responsibility, and so that there may be no excuses later on the grounds that the matter [initially] was of no importance. The principle to be followed is that all shall approve matters which concern all: let the judgment of all decide the future of all.

— Document No. 15 —

PTOLEMY OF LUCCA'S DISTINCTION BETWEEN POLITICAL AND REGAL LORDSHIP, 1298-1308 [26]

[26] Ptolemy of Lucca's *De regimine principum,* Book II, Chapter 8. Reprinted from *Medieval Political Ideas* by Ewart Lewis, by permission of Alfred A. Knopf, Inc. Copyright 1954 by Ewart Lewis. Ptolemy (1240-1327) was a Dominican and continuator of the work by Thomas Aquinas, with whom he was closely associated.

. . . . In his *Politics* [Bk. I, Ch. I], Aristotle has described two kinds of government: . . . namely, the political and the despotic. Political government is that in which a region, province, or town, or a citadel, is ruled by one or more men in accordance with its own statutes, as occurs in the regions of Italy and as particularly occurred in Rome, which was ruled by senators and consuls for the greater part of its history after the city was founded. . . . In such a lordship there are two reasons why the subjects cannot be so rigorously controlled as in a regal lordship. One reason is that the government of the ruler is temporary, and as a result his interest in those subjected to him is lessened by the consideration that his lordship will soon be at an end. . . . Moreover, political lordship is mercenary, for political rulers are attracted through salaries. Now, where payment is provided, rulers give less zealous attention to the governing of their subjects, and consequently the rigour of their discipline is moderated. . . . The second reason why political lordship is necessarily moderate and exercised with moderation concerns the subjects, since their disposition is naturally proportionate to such a system. For Ptolemy proves in the *Quadripartitus* that in regard to systems of morals the regions of men are distinguished in accordance with various constellations. . . . Thus the regions of the Romans which he places under Mars, are less easily brought to subjection. . . . Moreover, the self-confidence of the subjects, whether because they have been free of the lordship of rulers or because they have had experience of governing one another in turn, makes them bold for liberty and unwilling to bow their necks to rulers; thus political lordship is necessarily gentle. Furthermore, this form of ruling is in accordance with the form of the communal or municipal laws by which the ruler is bound; thus, because the prince is not free, his discretion is eliminated and is less like the divine providence. . . .

— Document No. 16 —

SELECTIONS FROM MARSIGLIO OF PADUA'S *DEFENSOR PACIS* 1324[27]

3. Let us moreover say, truly in accordance with the opinion of Aristotle in III *Politics,* ch. II, that the legislator, or prime and proper effective cause of law, is the people or body of citizens, or its more weighty part, through its choice or will orally expressed in the general assembly of citizens, commanding or determining, in regard to the civil actions of men, that something be done or not done, under penalty of temporal punishment. The more weighty part, I say, taking into consideration the number and the quality of persons in that community for which the law is enacted. The whole corporation of citizens, or its weightier part, either makes law itself, directly, or entrusts this task to some person or persons, who are not and cannot be the legislator in the absolute sense, but only for specific matters, and temporarily, and by virtue of the authority of the prime legislator. And I say in consequence that laws and anything whatever that is established by choice ought to receive the necessary approval by none other than that same prime legislator, with whatever solemnities may be appropriate. . . . And I further say that by that same authority laws, and other things that are established by choice, ought to undergo addition or diminution or total change, interpretation, and suspension, in accordance with the exigency of times or places or other circumstances which make such change

[27] From Dictio I, Ch. XII, sections 3, 4, 6, 7; Ch. XIII, section 8 of the *Defensor Pacis.* Reprinted from *Medieval Political Ideas* by Ewart Lewis, by permission from Alfred A. Knopf, Inc. Copyright 1954 by Ewart Lewis. Marsiglic Mainardino (1270-1342) was Rector of the University of Paris and a distinguished imperialist publicist for Louis of Bavaria in his struggle with Pope John XXII.

expedient for the sake of the common welfare. Also, by that same authority laws ought to be promulgated or proclaimed after their institution, so that no delinquent citizen or sojourner can plead ignorance of the law as his excuse.

4. Moreover, following Aristotle's opinion in III *Politics,* chs. 1, 3, 13, I mean by citizen any man who participated in the civil community, in the principate or the council or the jury, according to his rank. By this definition boys, slaves, sojourners, and women are excluded from the category of citizens, though in different ways. For the sons of citizens are potentially citizens, lacking only the qualification of age. And the weightier part should be discovered in accordance with the opinion of Aristotle in VI *Politics,* ch. 3. . . .

6. We may also prove the principal conclusion in this way. The authority of legislation belongs only to him whose making of the laws results in their being better or more directly observed. Now this is none other than the corporation of citizens; therefore to it belongs the authority of legislation. The first premise of this syllogism is very nearly self-evident, for a law would be idle if it were not observed. Whence Aristotle says in IV *Politics,* ch. 6, 'Moreover, to have good laws enacted and yet not to obey them does not constitute a good disposition of laws.' And he also says in VI *Politics,* ch. 5, 'There is no advantage if judgments concerning just things have been made and yet do not attain their end.' The minor premise I prove thus. Any one of the citizens will better observe that law which he seems to have imposed upon himself; such is the law laid down by the knowledge and command of the whole multitude of citizens. The first premise of this auxiliary syllogism is almost self-evident: for, since 'the state is a community of free men,' as it is written in III *Politics,* ch. 4, every citizen ought to be free and not bear the despotism—that is, the lordship over slaves—of another. Now this would not be the case if some one or some few of the citizens should lay down the law by their own authority for the corporation of citizens; for thus those who made the law would be the despots of the others. And therefore the rest of the citizens—namely, the larger part—would bear such a law, however good it might be, with vexation or not at all, and would protest

against it on the grounds that they had been treated with contempt, and, not having been summoned to its making, they would in no way observe it. But if it were made by the knowledge and consent of all the multitude, even if it were less useful, each of the citizens would easily observe and endure it; because each would seem to have established it for himself, and therefore would have no protest against it, but would rather endure it with a calm mind. I also prove the minor premise of the primary syllogism in another way, as follows. The power to cause laws to be observed belongs to the one who alone has coercive power over transgressors; now this is the corporation or its more weighty part; therefore it alone has the authority of legislation. . . .

— Document No. 17 —

DANTE ON LIBERTY AND MONARCHY, 1310-1313 [28]

Also, the human race is at its best when it is most free. . . .

. . . Liberty is the greatest of God's gifts to human nature, since through liberty we are made happy as men here and as gods elsewhere. And, if this is so, who will not agree that the human race is at its best when it is most able to use this principle? But the human race is most free when it is under a monarch. To prove this, we must

[28] From the *De Monarchia*, Bk. I, Ch. XII. Reprinted from *Medieval Political Ideas* by Ewart Lewis, by permission of Alfred A. Knopf, Inc. Copyright 1954 by Ewart Lewis. The great poet Dante Alighieri (1265-1321) was a Florentine nobleman. He was a member of the White Guelfs, a very conservative, even Ghibelline party. He was exiled in 1302 on a charge of political crime.

know that that thing is most free which exists for its own
sake and not for the sake of another, as the Philosopher
says in his *Metaphysics*.[29] For that which exists for the
sake of something else is necessitated by that for whose
sake it exists: as a path is necessitated by its goal. If the
human race is under a single monarch, it exists for its
own sake and not for the sake of another; for only then
are the perverse polities democracies, oligarchies, and
tyrannies, which force the human race into servitude kept
under control, as is apparent to one who surveys them all,
and then kings will govern, and aristocracies who are also
called optimates, and people zealous of liberty. Because,
since a monarch, as we have already shown, most loves
mankind, he desires all men to become good, which cannot be the case in a perverse polity. . . . Therefore the
human race is at its best when under a monarch; whence
it follows that monarchy is necessary for the well-being of
the world.

— Document No. 18 —

BARTOLUS ON POLITICAL PARTIES, c. 1340[30]

In regard to the third question: whether it is lawful
to have these parties [Guelph and Ghibelline], I say that
if a number of persons belong to a party or if a person
attaches himself to one party, not for the public good,
but for their own advantage or in order that they may

[29] As always, the Philosopher is Aristotle.
[30] From Bartolus, *De Guelphis,* Ch. III. Reprinted by permission of the publishers from Ephraim Emerton, *Humanism
   and Tyranny* (Cambridge, Mass.: Harvard University Press
   1925), pp. 277-80. Bartolus of Sassoferrato (1314-1357)
   was one of the most famous of all medieval jurists.

oppress others, that is absolutely unlawful. And, if several combine together to this end, this is punishable as if they had formed a conspiracy to the injury of an innocent person. If, however, there is one party in a city tending mainly to the common good in order that the place may be well and peaceably governed, and if it be impossible to hold the opposition in check without using a party name, then I think such a party organization is, generally speaking, lawful. . . .

If, however, one party wishes not only to resist, but to depose those who have the government in their hands, then, if they should rise against this government, that would be absolutely unlawful. But, if the existing government be a wicked and tyrannical one, then, since this is a government by one party, it is lawful that there should be another party as an opposition: first, if they have appealed to the overlord and have found that he cannot depose the tyrant without great difficulty and second, because the opposition would be acting for the public good, to the end that the order of the community may be restored. If, however, they should take this action to drive out the ruling party and set up a new tyranny of their own, then the opposite is true.

The first proposition is proved because it is lawful for men to execute justice on their own authority if no judge is at hand; and if this is lawful for the advantage of individuals, it is lawful for the deliverance of the Republic, for the defense of which everyone is responsible. Furthermore, if this is permitted against a destroyer of crops or a deserter from the army, far more ought it to be allowable against those who would destroy the Republic and bring it into servitude to themselves. The second point is proved, because it is not lawful to act for one's own private advantage. Those who have possession of the Republic by way of tyranny have acquired their rule either from the Republic itself or from the overlord or from some private source. Therefore another person who should wish to depose the tyranny for his own advantage would seem to act unlawfully. . . .

— Document No. 19 —

MID-FOURTEENTH CENTURY. BARTOLUS ON TYRANNY[31]

In this eighth chapter I take up the question of the tyrant *ex parte exercitii,* that is, as shown by his conduct. Even though his title be sound he is none the less a tyrant. I say that he is a tyrant because he rules "tyrannically," that is, his actions are not directed toward the common good but to his own advantage, and that means to rule unjustly—as is the case *de facto* in Italy. But now, that the method of proof may be made more clear, let us come down to specific acts which for the most part consist in the oppression of subjects.

These acts are clearly enumerated by the famous Plutarch in his *de regimine principum* under ten headings. First, it is the practice of tyrants to cause the ruin of powerful and distingushed men of the community, so that they cannot rebel against them; for we see that they murder even their brothers and blood relations, and that is an indication of the very worst kind of tyranny. Second, they banish their wise men, lest they discover and attack their iniquities and stir up the people against them. Third, they not only cause the ruin of study and education, but they prevent the training of capable men because they are always in fear of detection by wisdom. Fourth, they forbid private associations [*specialitates*] and public meetings, even lawful ones, through fear of uprisings. Fifth, they keep a multitude of informers about the place; for the man who is conscious of wrongdoing always believes that people are speaking ill of him and plotting against him,

[31] From Bartolus *Tractatus de Tyrannia,* Ch. VIII. Reprinted by permission of the publishers from Ephraim Emerton, *Humanism and Tyranny* (Cambridge, Mass.: Harvard University Press, 1925), pp. 140-44.

and for this reason he gladly listens to such informers. Sixth, the tyrant keeps the community in a state of division, so that each part may be in fear of the rest and so may not rebel against him. Seventh, the tyrant takes pain to keep his subjects poor, so that they may be fully occupied with getting their living and have no time for plotting against him. Eighth, he provokes wars and sends his fighting men abroad to prevent them from hatching plots and because through wars men are kept poor and withdrawn from study, which is what a tyrant desires. Also, in this way he keeps soldiers in training for his own use in time of need. Ninth, he makes up his bodyguard, not from citizens but from foreigners, for he stands in fear of his own countrymen. Tenth, when there are factions in the city he always attaches himself to one of them in order to break up the other.

Such are the opinions of Plutarch, and now let us examine them. First: To cause the ruin of specially capable persons, even of a brother, is a tyrannical act. This is true unless it be for a just cause, as, for example, in the case of Romulus and Remus. For who can doubt that if any powerful person in a city creates disturbance or sedition he ought to be banished by any just judge? If then the cause be a just one that act is not that of a tyrant. Second, the same rule applies to the ruining of wise men, if the cause be just. Third, the destruction of study and education: I understand this to apply to such pursuits as are suited to the [given] community. If, however, a ruler breaks up such pursuits as are not adapted to the community, this is not the act of a tyrant. Fourth, that assemblies, even lawful ones, are not permitted: If an offence is once committed by them it is certainly right to dissolve them; for I have known persons to come together under a pretense of religion and straightway to throw the town into confusion. We must, therefore, judge by the kind of persons assembled whether it is the act of a tyrant to break up a lawful assembly. Fifth, the keeping of informers in a city: This may be the act of a just ruler if it be done for a lawful purpose. A good ruler may employ informers to punish crimes and other offences in the community; but a tyrant uses them against those who may injure his own position and therefore his act concerns only his own advantage. Sixth, that the tyrant strives to foment divisions in the city: This is a tyrannical act, seeing that it is a primary duty of a just ruler to keep the peace among the citizens. Seventh, deliberately keeping the people in poverty is plainly an act of tyranny; for the good ruler cannot properly take anything for himself nor afflict his subjects with burdens upon either their persons or their property. Eighth, that incitement to civil war is in itself (*simplicite*) a tyrannical act: Sometimes a civil way may be a just war, but an unjust war is an act of tyranny pure and simple. Ninth, maintaining a bodyguard of non-citizens may be a just measure; for a people may be so uncontrollable and so obstinate that the ruler, just though he be, cannot rely upon them. This is especially apt to occur in a newly recovered territory, even under a just master. For this reason emperors sometimes drove out the inhabitants of a city and settled them elsewhere. So also we sometimes see good rulers building fortifications or collecting munitions in a city where their rule is a lawful one. But such things, in the case of a just ruler are due to some exceptional cause, whereas with a tyrant they are of ordinary occurrence. Tenth, adhering to one faction and oppressing another is an act of tyranny pure and simple, since the final purpose of a commonwealth is the peace and good order of the citizens—as has been said.

All the above, then, are indications whereby a tyranny can be proved, and especially these two: the promoting of divisions in the community and the impoverishment of citizens and abusing them in their persons or in their property. All this has been abundantly shown in the preceding chapters. From what has there been said it is evident what a tyranny is.

— Document No. 20 —

COLUCCIO SALUTATI ON CAESAR AS PRINCE OR TYRANT, 1400[32]

The fact is, their struggle was not as to whether some one man should rule and be the supreme dictator of the state, but which of the two it should be. For not only were standards set against standards, eagles against eagles, weapons against weapons, all of the same kind, but on both sides were also equal disloyalty, equal fury and self-seeking, an equal desire to oppress the citizens, to set aside the laws and to think anything right which was pleasing and profitable to the victors. It was a fight, not to maintain the Republic, but to destroy it. "Which cause was the better, it is forbidden to know," says the poet. Now, when the citizens, divided into hostile camps, determined to settle by force which should rule, it came to pass by the will of God that Caesar conquered. No one will deny that he atoned for the horrors of civil strife, than which nothing can be more cruel, by his wonderful magnanimity. For, as Cicero says: "He conquered, yet did not excite hatred in his good fortune, but rather allayed it by his leniency." Speaking of his geniality and his gentleness of nature the Man of Arpinum[33] did not hesitate to say: "We saw thy victory decided by the fortune of war; thy sword we have never seen unsheathed within the City. The citizens whom we have lost perished in the heat of

---

[32] From Chapter III of the *De Tyranno*. Reprinted by permission of the publishers from Ephraim Emerton, *Humanism and Tyranny* (Cambridge, Mass.: Harvard University Press, 1925), pp. 98-99. Salutati (1331-1406) was a distinguished Florentine humanist.

[33] Cicero.

battle, not in the fury of victory; so that no one can doubt that Caesar if he could, would call many of them back from the realm below. In fact he is protecting as many of the hostile party as he can."

Who then can think the rule of a man of such a character, such sentiments and such deeds as these, ought to be called a tyranny? But you ask me to give it a name. Hear then what Seneca—whom some call Florus—says. In his compendium of Roman history, after describing Caesar's wars, he concludes as follows: "Here at last was an end of fighting, a bloodless peace, a war counterbalanced by clemency. No one was put to death by order of the commander except Afranius, to whom he had once before been sufficiently indulgent, Faustus Sulla— Pompey had taught him to be afraid of sons-in-law— and the daughter of Pompey together with her children by Sulla. In this case he was taking precautions for the future.

So that, with the approval of the citizens, all kinds of honors were heaped upon this one man: statues around the temples, in the theatre a pointed crown, a raised seat in the Senate, decorated gable for his house, his name given to a month of the year; besides these the titles of "Father of the Fatherland" and "Perpetual Dictator"; finally—whether by his own consent or not is uncertain —the insignia of royalty offered him publicly by Antony as Consul. Can a man raised to power constitutionally and through his own merits, a man who showed such a humane spirit, not to his own partisans alone, but also to his opponents because they were his fellow citizens— can he properly be called a tyrant? I do not see how this can be maintained, unless indeed we are to pass judgment without clear definitions.

We may, therefore, conclude with this proposition: that Caesar was not a tyrant, seeing that he held his principate in a commonwealth, lawfully and not in abuse of law.

IV PRINCELY PRIVILEGES AND CUSTOMS

— Document No. 21 —

OTTO I GRANTS A MARKET TO THE ARCHBISHOP OF HAMBURG, 965 [34]

In the name of the undivided Trinity. Otto by the favor of God Emperor, Augustus. If we grant the requests of clergymen and liberally endow the places which are dedicated to the worship of God, we believe that it will undoubtedly assist in securing for us the eternal reward. Therefore, let all know that for the love of God we have granted the petition of Adaldagus, the reverend archbishop of Hamburg, and have given him permission to establish a market in the place called Bremen. In connection with the market we grant him jurisdiction, tolls, a mint, and all other things connected therewith to which our royal treasury would have a right. We also take under our special protection all the merchants who live in that place, and grant them the same protection and rights as those merchants have who live in other royal cities. And no one shall have any jurisdiction there except the aforesaid archbishop and those to whom he may delegate it. Signed with our hand and sealed with our ring.

[34] From Altmann and Bernheim, *Ausgewahlte Urkunden* (Berlin, 1904), translated in *A Source Book for Medieval History* by Oliver J. Thatcher and Edgar Holmes McNeal, copyright 1905 by Charles Scribner's Sons, 1933. Reprinted with the permission of the publisher.

— Document No. 22 —

THE BISHOP OF HAMBURG GRANTS A CHARTER TO COLONISTS, 1106[35]

1. In the name of the holy and undivided Trinity. Frederick, by the grace of God bishop of Hamburg, to all the faithful in Christ, gives a perpetual benediction. We wish to make known to all the agreement which certain people living this side of the Rhine, who are called Hollanders, have made with us.

2. These men came to us and earnestly begged us to grant them certain lands in our bishopric, which are uncultivated, swampy, and useless to our people. We have consulted our subjects about this and, considering that this would be profitable to us and to our successors, have granted their request.

3. The agreement was made that they should pay us every year one *denarius* for every hide of land. We have thought it necessary to determine the dimensions of the hide, in order that no quarrel may hereafter arise about it. The hide shall be 720 royal rods long and thirty royal rods wide. We also grant them the streams which flow through this land.

4. They agreed to give the tithe according to our decree, that is, every eleventh sheaf of grain, every tenth lamb, every tenth pig, every tenth goat, every tenth goose, and a tenth of the honey and of the flax. For every colt they shall pay a *denarius* on St. Martin's day, and for every calf an obol.[36]

5. They promised to obey me in all ecclesiastical matters

[35] *Ibid.*, pp. 572-73.
[36] A *denarius* is a penny; an obol a halfpenny. But they were much more valuable than these terms convey today.

according to the decrees of the holy fathers, the canonical law, and the practice in the diocese of Utrecht.

6. They agreed to pay every year two marks for every 100 hides for the privilege of holding their own courts for the settlement of all their differences about secular matters. They did this because they feared they would suffer from the injustice of foreign judges. If they cannot settle the more important cases they shall refer them to the bishop. And if they take the bishop with them [that is, from Hamburg to the colony] for the purpose of deciding one of their trials, they shall provide for his support as long as he remains there by granting him one-third of all the fees arising from the trial; and they shall keep the other two-thirds.

7. We have given them permission to found churches wherever they may wish on these lands. For the support of the priests who shall serve God in these churches we grant a tithe of our tithes from these parish churches. . . .

— Document No. 23 —

THE CUSTOMS OF NEWCASTLE-UPON-TYNE IN THE TIME OF HENRY I, 1068-1135 [37]

These are the laws and customs which the burgesses of Newcastle-upon-Tyne had in the time of Henry, king of England, and which they still have by right:

The burgesses may distrain foreigners within their market and without, and within their homes and without, and within their borough and without, and they may do this without the permission of the reeve,[38] unless the

---

[37] From *English Historical Documents, 1042-1189,* edited by D. C. Douglas and G. W. Greenway. Reprinted by permission of Oxford University Press, Inc.

[38] The reeve was the chief magistrate, a royal officer.

courts are being held within the borough, or unless they are in the field on army service, or are doing castle-guard. But a burgess may not distrain on another burgess without the permission of the reeve.

If a burgess shall lend anything in the borough to someone dwelling outside, the debtor shall pay back the debt if he admit it, or otherwise do right in the court of the borough.

Pleas which arise in the borough shall there be held and concluded except those which belong to the king's crown.

If a burgess shall be sued in respect of any plaint he shall not plead outside the borough except for defect of court; nor need he answer, except at a stated time and place, unless he has already made a foolish answer, or unless the case concerns matters pertaining to the crown.

If a ship comes to the Tyne and wishes to unload, it shall be permitted to the burgesses to purchase what they please. And if a dispute arises between a burgess and a merchant, it shall be settled before the third tide.

Whatever merchandise a ship brings by sea must be brought to the land; except salt and herring which must be sold on board ship.

If anyone has held land in burgage for a year and a day justly and without challenge, he need not answer any claimant, unless the claimant is outside the kingdom of England, or unless he be a boy not having the power of pleading.

If a burgess have a son in his house and at his table, his son shall have the same liberty as his father.

If a villein come to reside in the borough, and shall remain as a burgess in the borough for a year and a day, he shall thereafter always remain there, unless there was a previous agreement between him and his lord for him to remain there for a certain time.

If a burgess sues anyone concerning anything, he cannot force the burgess to trial by battle, but the burgess must defend himself by his oath, except in a charge of treason when the burgess must defend himself by battle. Nor shall a burgess offer battle against a villein unless he has first quitted his burgage.

No merchant except a burgess can buy wool or hides or other merchandise outside the town, nor shall he buy them within the town except from burgesses.

If a burgess incurs forfeiture he shall give 6 *oras*[39] to the reeve.

In the borough there is no 'merchet' nor 'heriot' nor 'bloodwite' nor 'stengesdint'. . . .[40]

— Document No. 24 —

THE LIBERTIES OF TOULOUSE, 1147[41]

Let it be known to all men living and to be born that I Alphonse, Count of Toulouse, proclaim, recognize, and grant that in no way do I have tallage or tolls in the city of Toulouse, nor in the suburb of St. Sernin, nor against the men and woman living there or who will live there, nor shall I have in the said city the right to summon the militia to campaign unless war be waged against me in Toulouse, nor shall I make any loan there unless it should be the lender's wish. Wherefore I confirm and commend to all citizens of Toulouse and its suburb, present and future, all their good customs and privileges, those they now enjoy and which I may give and allow to them. All this, as it is written above, Raymond of St. Gilles, son of the said count, approves and grants.

[39] An *ora* equaled 16 to 20 pence.
[40] Taxes on marriage, on movables at death, and upon high crime involving effusion of blood or assault.
[41] From the *Cartulary of the Bourg,* published in R. Limouzin-Lamothe, *La commune de Toulouse* (Toulouse-Paris, 1932), p. 263.

— Document No. 25 —

SELECTIONS FROM THE CUSTOMS OF LORRIS, 1155 [42]

1. Everyone who has a house in the parish of Lorris shall pay as *cens*[43] sixpence only for his house, and for each acre of land that he possesses in the parish.

2. No inhabitant of the parish of Lorris shall be required to pay a toll or other tax on his provisions; and let him not be made to pay measurage fee on the grain which he has raised by his own labor.

3. No burgher shall go on an expedition, on foot or on horseback, from which he cannot return the same day to his home if he so desires.

4. No burgher shall pay toll on the road to Etampes, to Orléans, to Milly (which is in the Gatinais), or to Melun.

5. No one who has property in the parish of Lorris shall forfeit it for any offense whatsoever, unless the offense shall have been committed against us or any of our *Hotes*.[44]

6. No person while on his way to the fairs and markets of Lorris, or returning, shall be arrested or disturbed, unless he shall have committed an offense on the same day. . . .

9. No one, neither we nor any other, shall exact from the burghers of Lorris, any tallage, tax, or subsidy.

12. If a man shall have a quarrel with another, but without breaking into a fortified house, and if the parties shall have reached an agreement without bringing suit before the provost, no fine shall be due to us or our provost on account of the affair. . . .

---

[42] From M. Prou, *Les coutumes de Lorris* (Paris, 1884), translated in F. A. Ogg, *A Source Book in Medieval History* (New York, 1907/35), pp. 328-30. These customs were widely copied in the French royal domain.

[43] Rent.

[44] Literally, Guests, referring to the settlers of Lorris.

15. No inhabitant of Lorris is to render us the obligation of *corvée*,[45] except twice a year, when our wine is to be carried to Orléans, and not elsewhere. . . .

35. We ordain that every time there shall be a change of provosts in the town the new provost shall take an oath faithfully to observe these regulations; and the same thing shall be done by new sergeants every time that they are installed.[46]

— Document No. 26 —

ROYAL PRIVILEGE TO LONDON, 1155[47]

Henry, king of the English, and duke of the Normans, and of the men of Aquitaine, count of the Angevins, to the archbishops, bishops, abbots, earls, barons, justiciars, sheriffs, and all his servants and liegemen of England, both French and English, greeting. Know that I have granted to my citizens of London that none of them shall plead outside the walls of the city of London, except respecting holdings outside the city, and in respect of my moneyers and my servants. I have also granted to them quittance from the murder fine both within the city and in the Portsoken;[48] and that none of them shall be tried by battle; and that in respect of pleas of the crown they may make their proof according to the ancient

[45] Obligatory service and labor.
[46] The provost was the royal magistrate or officer similar to the English reeve mentioned above. The sergeants were police and lesser officers.
[47] From *English Historical Documents, 1042-1189,* edited by D. C. Douglas and G. W. Greenway. Reprinted by permission of Oxford University Press, Inc.
[48] Jurisdiction of the chartered borough.

custom of the city; and that within the walls no one shall be forcibly billeted, or by the assignment of the marshall. I have also granted that all the citizens of London shall be quit of toll and estage[49] through all England and in every harbour; and that no one of them shall be fined at discretion except according to the law of the city which they had in the time of king Henry, my grandfather. And in no plea in the city shall there be 'miskenning',[50] nor shall the hustings court be held more than once a week.[51] I grant further that they shall have their lands and pledges and debts whoever owes them; and that right shall be done them according to the law of the city respecting their lands and tenures within the city; and that pleas respecting all their debts contracted in London, and respecting pledges there taken, shall be held in London. And if anyone in all England shall take toll or custom from the men of London, and shall refuse them satisfaction, then shall the sheriff of London take a surety respecting it within London. I also grant to them that they shall have their chases wherever they had them in the time of King Henry, my grandfather. Further, in respect of payments made by the city, I grant that they shall be quit of 'brudtolle' and of 'childwyte' and of 'jeresgieve' and of 'scotale',[52] so that neither my sheriff of London nor any other bailiff shall exact 'scotale'. The aforesaid customs I grant them, and all other liberties and free customs as well as ever they had them in the time of King Henry, my grandfather. Wherefore I will, and firmly order that they and their heirs shall have and hold them by hereditary right from me and my heirs.

[49] Tax on ship lading.
[50] Slips of tongue when repeating legal formulas in court.
[51] The borough court presided over by a royal officer or reeve.
[52] Pontage, fine for impregnating female villeins, payment for right of burgage, and forced contributions to royal officers.

— Document No. 27 —

THE PEACE OF BÉZIERS, c. 1170[53]

Bernard, by the grace of God Bishop of Béziers, to his beloved Viduino archpriest of Béziers, greeting. . . . We, indeed, ever so much disturbed over the everpresent wars and calamities, have faith in the mercy of God, and wish to restore with His help the peace and prosperity of the land.

Wherefore we have summoned the viscount R. and the knights of the region and made them swear a peace. The following are understood to be protected by this peace: all religious and their property; all secular clergy and their property; all peasants and their property; all fishermen and hunters; women and their unarmed retainers; all those who go to mourn the dead; also, all unshod horses, and all pack animals whoever they may be, and all these goods they are carrying; all travelers and merchants with their goods; cows, oxen, pigs and goats; flour mills and wine presses.

Wherefore, by our authority we enjoin that you warn your parishioners to swear allegiance to the peace until the first Sunday before Easter, and to follow the regulations of the peace, and to force those who may infringe it to come before us at Sarzac, whenever they may be cited, that they be strongly reminded of it. And if any lord of a castle should disdain to observe this peace until the aforementioned Sunday, the divine office shall not be celebrated on his lands until he swears observance. All above the age of fifteen shall swear unless they wish to be rejected by the Church. In this manner shall you

[53] From C. Devic and J. Vaisette, *Histoire générale de Languedoc* (Toulouse, 1879), vol. VIII, col. 275-76. It is interesting that viscount Raymond—not the bishop—was the lord of Béziers.

warn the rectors of the churches subordinate to the Bishop of Béziers. . . .

We also decree that from sunset Thursday until dawn Monday all those who go about unarmed shall rest under the protection of the peace so that no one shall dare to seize them, beat them, or in any way cause them injury.

— Document No. 28 —

CHARTER OF HENRY II TO DUBLIN, 1171-1172 [54]

Henry, king of the English, duke of the Normans and of the men of Aquitaine, count of Anjou, to his archbishops, bishops, abbots, earls, barons, justiciars, sheriffs, servants, and to his liegemen, French, English, and Irish, of all his land, greeting. Know that I have given and granted to my men of Bristol my city of Dublin to inhabit. Wherefore I will, and firmly order, that these should inhabit and hold it from me and from my heirs, freely and quietly, fully and wholly, and honourably, with all the liberties and free customs which the men of Bristol have at Bristol and throughout my land. Witness. . . . At Dublin.

[54] From *English Historical Documents 1042-1189*, edited by D. C. Douglas and G. W. Greenway. Reprinted by permission of Oxford University Press, Inc.

— Document No. 29 —

DIVISION OF THE SEIGNORY OF THE TOWN OF ARRAS BETWEEN THE BISHOP AND THE COUNT OF FLANDERS, 1177[55]

Given the disagreements which are wont to arise over contracts and agreements because of the uncertain memory of man. . . . I Fumaldus, by God's grace Bishop of Artois, and I Philip, Count of Flanders and Vermandois, compose this agreement with regard to the dispute we have over our rights, especially those relating to secular jurisdiction; and we certify this agreement with our seals. In the past there have been many disputes between our predecessors; in our time, with the consent and by the express wish of the chapter of Artois and of the men of the count, we declare the disputes terminated by this solution.

All litigation involving 60 *solidi*[56] or less which may arise in the area bounded by the Strate gate and the Tenard bridge, and within the walls throughout the entire quarter, shall be subject to the justice of the bishop. This applies to all cases. Understood also are the breaking of all prohibitions, no matter by whom; the falsifying of all measures, and cheating in the measurement of cloth and all other things with the exception of counterfeiting, perjury or corrupting judges and cases of dueling also shall be the bishops. . . .

Done in the year of our Lord, 1177.

[55] From Georges Espinas and Henri Pirenne, *Recueil des documents relatifs a l'histoire de l'industrie drapière en Flandres* (Brussels, 1906), vol. I, p. 113-14.
[56] Shillings.

— Document No. 30 —

A SELECTION FROM THE TREATY OF CONSTANCE BETWEEN FREDERICK I AND THE LOMBARD TOWNS, 1183 [57]

We, Frederick, Emperor of the Romans, and Henry, our son, King of the Romans, grant to you cities, places, and persons of the League, your royal rights and customs, both in the city and outside the city of Verona, its castle and suburbs, and in other places, cities and persons of the League forever; namely that in that city you shall have all the things which you have, or have had hitherto; and outside the city you shall enjoy without contradiction all the customs which you exercise or have exercised from of old, namely in the *fodrum*,[58] groves, pastures, bridges, streams, and mills, just as you have or have had them in the past, and in the army, and in fortifying the cities, in jurisdiction both in criminal and in financial matters, both within and without the city, and in other things which are of convenience to the cities. . . .

[57] From *Documenti di Storia Italiana,* ed. M. Tabarrani (Florence, 1876), vol. VI, translated in R. C. Cave and H. H. Coulson, *A Source Book for Medieval Economic History* (Milwaukee, 1936), pp. 205-06.
[58] The right of hospitality or quartering usually paid in kind.

THE IMPERIAL DIET ON THE ESTABLISHMENT OF TOWN COUNCILS IN EPISCOPAL CITIES, 1218 [59]

In the name of the holy and undivided Trinity. Frederick II, by the favor of God king of the Romans, Augustus, and king of Sicily. . . . Our beloved prince, Henry, bishop of Basel, came into the presence of us and of many princes, barons, and nobles of the empire and demanded a decision about the following matter, namely: Whether we or anyone else had the right to establish a council in a city [that is, to give a city municipal freedom] which was subject to a bishop, without the bishop's consent and permission. We first asked our beloved prince, Theodoric, the venerable archbishop of Trier, about this, and he, after some deliberation, declared that we neither could nor should grant or establish a council in the city of the aforesaid bishop of Basel without the consent of him or of his successors. The question was then asked in due form of all who were present, both princes, nobles, and barons, and they confirmed the decision of the archbishop of Trier. We also, as a just judge, approve this decision, and declare it to be right. We therefore remove and depose the council which is now in Basel, and we annul the charter which we granted the people of Basel authorizing the establishment of this council, and they shall never make any further use of it. As a greater evi-

[59] From Altmann and Bernheim, *Ausgewahlte Urkunden* (Berlin, 1904), translated in *A Source Book for Medieval History* by Oliver J. Thatcher and Edgar Holmes McNeal, copyright 1905 by Charles Scribner's Sons, 1933 by Oliver J. Thatcher. Reprinted with the permission of the publisher.

dence of our favor and love for the aforesaid bishop of
Basel, we forbid, under the threat of the loss of our favor,
the people of Basel to make or set up a council or any
constitution, by whatever name it may be called, without
the consent and permission of their bishop. . . .

— Document No. 32 —

ROYAL EXEMPTION FROM ALL TOLLS GIVEN THE TOWN OF BARCELONA, 1232[60]

In the name of the Lord Jesus Christ. Be it known to
all, both present and future, that we, James, by the grace
of God, King of Aragon, and of the kingdom of Majorca,
Count of Barcelona and Urgell and Lord of Montpellier,
mindful of the many and praiseworthy services and kind-
nesses, which you, our beloved and faithful citizens of
Barcelona, have always shown to us and to our predecessors, and which, with faith and devotion, you freely show
today, and wishing to show you special favor, the benefit
of which both you and yours may enjoy forever, we,
therefore, by this charter given on behalf of us and our
successors, enfranchise and make free in every way each
and all of our beloved citizens, both now and in the future,
the inhabitants of Barcelona, with all your goods and
merchandise from all tolls, bridge tolls, municipal tolls,
and all tolls and customs, new and old, decreed or to be
decreed, and from all taxes on your goods everywhere
throughout all places in our kingdoms and lands and all

[60] From A. De Capmany, *Memorias historicas sobre la marina,
comercio y artes de la antigua ciudad de Barcelona* (Mad-
rid, 1779), vol. II, p. 13, translated in Cave and Coulson,
A Source Book for Medieval Economic History, pp. 215-
16. The marabotin was a Spanish silver coin of Arabic
origin.

places under our dominion, both by land and sea, and on the river, and going from, staying at, or returning to the harbor. Therefore we decree and firmly ordain that no toll-gatherer, collector, tax-gatherer, prefect, majordomo, treasurer, justiciar, justice or judge, alcalde, mayor or bailiff, or any other official of ours, or servant, present or future, shall impede, take, or detain you, or any one of you or your officials or messengers or any of your goods or merchandise, in any place, by reason of those things from which, as we have said, we have enfranchised you and yours, but you shall be free, exempt, and quit of all the said things everywhere, always, and to the innermost parts of our kingdom. And whoever, against the tenor of this our charter, shall attempt to tax you, or your servants or messengers, or your goods or merchandise, which you have or shall have in the future, let him know that he will have incurred without any remedy both our anger and a penalty of 1000 marabotins, to his cost and at his expense, and that he must make restitution to you fully and in double. Given at Barcelona on the 12th of April, in the year of the Lord, 1232.

— Document No. 33 —

MILITARY SERVICE OWED BY CITIZENS OF AVIGNON TO THE COUNT OF PROVENCE AND THE COUNT OF TOULON AND AVIGNON, 1251 [61]

Likewise, the said citizens shall perform military service at the command of the lords or their vicars once a year for eleven days . . . wherever it may please the lord

[61] From M. A. R. de Maulde, *Coutumes et règlements de la République d'Avignon* (Paris, 1879), p. 269.

counts or their court, to the distance of twenty leagues
from the city of Avignon. They cannot be forced to go
personally, and may send knights, mercenaries, or replacements to do service. If, however, the said knights,
mercenaries, or stand-ins do not have proper horses, they
must either make the necessary arrangements in some way
or go, unless they can offer a reasonable excuse. Moreover, honorable burghers who are wont to live in the style
of knights enjoy the same privilege as above. Other
burghers, however, shall go on campaign unless they can
give a good excuse, or unless they be such for whom it
would be unseemly to fight on foot. And these, if they
send replacements, may also remain at home. Hereafter,
knights and other citizens with horse and arms on campaign or in the service of their lords or their deputies
shall go at their lords' expense, and the burghers and
knights shall receive the same stipend. This is to be
understood with respect to knights and burghers who do
not hold a fief of the said lords or of one of them, in
return for which they are to serve at their own expense.
Citizens cannot be compelled to give money in place of
campaign service.

V TOWN STATUTES
AND ORDINANCES

— Document No. 34 —

THE CONSTITUTION
AND CONSULATE
OF ARLES, 1142-55 [62]

If, in truth, public discussions should be held in the assembly with regard to changes in the consulate, changes of any kind in the communal custom, issues of war or of actions of reprisal to be taken in the public interest, and collections of taxes, then this discussion and council should be provided for the city and consulate upon the decision of the better and wiser part of the consulate and of the archbishop. And whatever they may determine shall be supported strongly and in good faith. . . . In this consulate there will be twelve consuls: four knights, four men from the bourg, two from the Mercato and two from the Borriano, and those who are in the commune shall be governed and ruled by these. And, the regime of the consulate having been established, the aforesaid shall have the power of justice, and their judgement shall be carried out in matters of personal injury, property, or indeed any other matters. . . . This consulate will signify peace, the restoration of the good old days, and the reformation of society. The churches, monasteries, and all places holy to God, the highways and public streets, the waters and the land, all will be governed by this peace.

[62] From Ch. Giraud, *Essai sur l'histoire du droit français au moyen-âge* (Paris, 1846), vol. II, p. 4.

And the peace will be sworn for a period of fifty years, and every five years all strangers and newcomers will swear to uphold it; and in this manner the consulate will be renewed and preserved; and the whole commune, maintained intact for service to God and for the public good, will be sustained and sworn to through the good offices of the archbishop. . . . If, indeed, civil discord of any kind should arise, no slinger or archer with stone or bow shall fight or attack others in the city or in the bourg. And no stranger shall be received in the commune without the wish and consent of the archbishop and of all the consuls.

— Document No. 35 —

DECREE OF THE COUNT OF TOULOUSE ON THE ELECTION OF THE CONSULS OF NIMES, 1198[63]

Let it be known to all men that I, Raymond, by the grace of God Duke of Narbonne, Count of Toulouse, Marquis of Provence, do state and decree that the consulate of Nimes shall be chosen in the following manner as long as it may please me and my heirs.

The entire population of the city or the greatest [possible] part of it will be assembled by crier and horn together with our representatives for the purpose of choosing consuls. And when they are all assembled, they shall elect from each of the districts into which the city is divided five good men, which twenty will swear to

[63] From Devic and Vaisette, *Histoire générale de Languedoc* (Toulouse, 1879), vol. VIII, col. 449-50.

choose to the best of their ability four consuls for the purpose of maintaining the safety and well-being of the city and of ourselves. And these four consuls-elect will swear that perpetually, in all their deliberations and actions, they will remember and maintain our welfare and the common good of the entire citizen body. And they will manifest their concern in their good judgment and good faith; and in all things will they follow their good conscience and sense of justice. Done this day . . . in the palace of the lord bishop of Nimes in the presence. . . .

— Document No. 36 —

FLORENTINE TAXATION, 1224 [64]

In the name of God, amen. We, Albert de Corsino, [etc.] elected and appointed by the common council of the Commune of Florence, in the time of the lordship of Inghirrami de Magreto, by the grace of God, Podestà of Florence, according to the mandate of the same Council gathered, according to custom, at the sound of the bell on March 20th in the palace of the Commune of Florence; at which council there were also present at the wish and command of the said Podestà the consuls of the merchants, bankers, of the *Arte della Lana*,[65] the priors of the crafts, and also twenty men from every *sestiere* of the city, in which Council it was said, confirmed, and agreed, that twelve men should be elected, two from each *sestiere*, who ought to have full power and authority over all the

---

[64] From *Documenti di Storia Italiana,* vol. X (Florence, 1896), translated in Cave and Coulson, *A Source Book for Medieval Economic History*, p. 12.

[65] The gild of the manufacturers or merchant-entrepreneurs of woolen cloth.

consuls who were in office when the tower of Semifonte
was destroyed, and over all other greater consuls of the
city, and over all court officials, castellans, syndics, pro-
curators, and prefects who have been in office from the
time of the said consuls up to the first of last January,
and over those who have and hold the new and old walls
of the city of Florence, and who keep them, and also over
those who have and hold the public squares of the Commune wherever they are and who keeps them; and over all
and each they should have full and free authority to speak,
pronounce, and impose (their commands) for clearing
the debt of the Commune of Florence; wherefore, we,
etc., impose, etc. The greater abbey of Florence, i.e., St.
Mary's for 166 fathoms of wall: L 191. 17 solidi 6
denarii.[66]

— Document No. 37 —

THE STATUTES
OF VOLTERRA, 1224 [67]

A. On the Election of the Consuls and the Podesta and How They Are to Be Summoned

If the person elected consul is not in the city of Volterra,
the consuls or the podestà should send for him, and they
may take whatever steps are necessary to do this. This
holds true for the podestà elect also. And whosoever may
be named consul will be asked by the consuls or the
podestà whether he will accept the office, and if he re-
jects it or refuses to swear to the consuls or the podestà

[66] 191 pounds, 17 shillings, and sixpence.
[67] *Statuti di Volterra*, ed. Enrico Fiumi (Florence, 1952), vol.
I, pp. 111, 113, 162-63, 214, 231-2. Volterra is in Tuscany.

that he will accept the consulship, the consuls or the podestà will then summon another to be consul instead. And they shall do this within three days of the refusal. But he who accepts the consulship, or promises that he will accept it, that man shall be consul. And he who serves as consul for a term will not be eligible again for the office for three years. Likewise, he who is podestà for a term shall not serve again as podestà until three years have passed.

B. On the Election of Officials for the Commune of Volterra

The new consuls or the podestà are bound to choose one good man who will choose two better and more suitable men whom he may know; and these will swear to choose for the commune, in good faith, six councillors, a treasurer, a notary, overseers, a treasurer of the customs house, and messengers, all good and true men.

C. On Not Changing the Constitution for a Year

No chapter of this constitution shall be changed for a whole year unless by certain constitutional experts who shall be chosen for this purpose, and these alone may change the constitution for the coming year. And we say that no emendation may be placed in the laws of the commune of Volterra save by these designated experts. These men shall be called before the full assembly of citizens or before the council where the advisors of the commune sit together with the consuls of the merchants and the lords of the district, or the majority of these, and where also there are 100 men of the town. And, when the experts are questioned, they should be questioned by the person who swore in good faith to choose them. And if any one of the consuls, or the podestà or any other person of this city or its territory should do otherwise, or cause the contrary to be done, he shall be fined 100 pounds; and the person who writes any illegal constitution will be fined 25 pounds and will lose his office for ten years. Moreover, when the consuls or the podestà believe that the constitution should be emended or changed for the following year, they should summon the constitutional experts three months before the expiration of their office.

D. With Regard to Anyone Making a Conspiracy Against the Commune

Should anyone order or make any organization or conspiracy or sworn association against the well-being of the commune of Volterra, he shall pay a fine of 50 pounds; and whoever writes this agreement will pay a fine of 10 pounds; and whoever joins this conspiracy or association will pay a fine of 100 shillings unless this should be done by the word of the consuls or the podestà with the consent of all or of the majority of them and of the consuls of the merchants.

E. Oath of the Citizens of Volterra

In the name of the Lord, amen. I, N, swear on the holy gospels of God to observe and fulfill and never violate by fraud each and every order which the consuls or podestà of Volterra should have me obey, during the term of their office, for the honor of the commune. Likewise, the advice which the consuls or the podestà may ask of me I shall give to the best of my ability, and in all honesty. Likewise, the confidence or secrets which may be made to me by the consuls or the podestà or by some other person in the name of the commune of Volterra, these trusts I shall hold and not violate save with the consent of the consuls or the podestà, lest he who trusted me be injured.

Likewise, if I should hear the great bell sound once the call to assembly I shall come to the public meeting without arms, and I shall remain in good faith until the end of the meeting, should there be one, and I shall not leave except by permission of the consuls or the podestà or their designated representative. Likewise, if I should hear the two great bells sounding the call to assembly I shall appear at the designated place armed, and shall not leave save by the express wish of the consuls or the podestà or their delegates. Likewise, if the said consuls or podestà should ask me, or if one of them should ask me for my tower or any other fortified place, I shall give it to them for their purposes, and I shall not take it back or attempt to take it back against their will. Likewise, I swear to help maintain the salt monopoly. And all this I swear to do and observe in good faith without deceit throughout the tenure of the consuls and the podestà. And let this document stand unaltered, and let nothing be added to it.

— Document No. 38 —

THE CUSTOMS OF AVIGNON, 1243[68]

A. ON STREETS AND BRIDGES

Likewise we decree that all public streets outside the city be widened and repaired so that they all shall be at least two *cannae* in width, and if anywhere roads or bridges or a lesser breadth are found, they shall be brought to the aforesaid measurement. The construction shall be done of the roads leading to the Rhone river from the episcopal tower, from St. Ruffo, from the tannery, from St. Verano and from St. Michael and from other places situated at a like distance . . . and if, perhaps, beyond these limits, there are found to be roads which are very narrow or which offer difficult passage, then these roads too shall be widened if the good and wise men, described below, should see fit. . . .

B. ON JEWS AND WHORES

Likewise, we declare that Jews or whores shall not dare to touch with their hands either bread or fruit put out for sale, and that if they should do this they must buy what they have touched.

. . . Likewise, we decree that no one shall have a water

[68] From M.A.R. de Maulde, *Coutumes et règlements de la République d'Avignon* (Paris, 1879), pp. 167, 170-71, 200.

pipe or pipes emptying into the public street through which water flows out onto the street . . . with the exception of rain water or well water. And if anyone should so offend, he shall pay a fine of five shillings for every offense.

Likewise, we decree that no one shall throw water onto the street, nor any steaming liquid, nor chaff, nor the refuse of grapes, nor human filth, nor bath water, nor indeed any dirt. Nor shall he throw anything into the street under his house nor allow his family to do so. . . . And he who commits this offense, be he head of the family or not, shall pay a fine of two shillings for every offense; and his accusor shall receive a third of the fine.

— Document No. 39 —

STATUTE ON THE CAPTAINCY OF GUIDO BONACOLSI IN MANTUA, 1299[69]

We declare and affirm that the distinguished lord Guido de Bonacolsis is and ought to be for all time captain general of the city and district of Mantua, and that he shall exercise that captaincy and rule and govern the territory and commune of Mantua with full, unalloyed, free, and general authority and freedom of will, and that he shall rule as seems best to him, with or without advice. And the said Guido, captain of Mantua, shall have full and unrestricted sovereignty, command, power, and seignorial rights and freedom of action in the commune, over the town, and over the men of the city and county

[69] From Ernst Salzer, *Über die Anfänge der Signorie in Oberitalien* (Berlin, 1900), pp. 302-03.

of Mantua. And he shall have this power that he may impose and remit taxes; engage in civil and criminal litigation or cause such to be started; order executions or order them to be held; compose agreements among allies; wage war; make truce and conclude peace; gain allies; join alliances; receive and restore the exiled; choose, establish and dismiss, condemn and absolve all podestas, judges, rectors, assessors, and all other officials; establish and withhold stipends; summon and assemble the wise men and consultative bodies of the town so that no assembly, dispute, convocation or public gathering may be held without his special or general permission. And he may, with or without the advice of these assemblies, make [constitutional] changes, establish ordinances, decrees, and statutes, and announce and interpret each and every thing which he deems involved with the welfare of the city and commune and citizenry of Mantua. And he shall do all this with or without advice as he sees fit, merely at the exercise of his own unlimited and sufficient discretion and will; nor shall he be bound by any law, custom, edict, decree, or statute. And the podesta and the rectors and their families and all other officials of the commune of Mantua are bound to acknowledge and observe whatever the lord captain Guido may say, lead them to do, or advise on any matter. . . .

STATUTES OF THE CAPTAIN OF THE PEOPLE IN FLORENCE, 1322-1325 [70]

A. On the Settlement of Disputes Which May Arise Among the Gilds

It is ordained and established that if one gild has a quarrel with another, the lord Captain and Defender of the time, together with the lord priors of the gilds and the Standard-bearer of justice, shall call a meeting and summon to his court the heads of the twelve principal gilds and place the issue before them. And whatever these twelve captains shall decide, the interested parties being absent from the deliberations, the Lord Captain and Defender shall force the conflicting parties to observe, under penalty and threat of banishment . . . applicable to the Lord Captain and Defender himself.

B. That At a Moment of Civil Danger No Magnate Shall Visit or Stay at the Home of Another

Likewise, it is established that on the day or night on which there is noise, tumult or public uprising in the city of Florence, within the city or without in the suburbs, no one of the magnates of the city, community or district of Florence, in any way or for any reason, shall dare or venture to go or stay, with or without arms, to the home or at the home of another magnate . . . of Florence. And if anyone should do so, he shall be punished . . . to the extent of 2,000 pounds for each offense. . . .

---

[70] From Lib. V, cap. V, LVI, LXVI of the Statuo del capitano del populo degli anni 1322-1325 published in Romolo Caggese, *Statuti della repubblica fiorentina* (Florence, 1910), vol. I, pp. 258-59.

C. That Magnates May Not Testify Against Members of the Popolo Without the Consent of the Priors

Because the magnates and powerful persons often bear false witness against the common people, it is ordained and established that no magnate may testify against any member of the popolo without permission of the lord Priors and the Standard-bearer of justice. And if anyone should bring testimony, it shall count for nothing, and whoever the magnate may be, he shall be punished, unless he has a license from the aforementioned officials, with a fine of 200 pounds.

— Document No. 41 —

A PLEBISCITE IN PROVINS, 1344-1356[71]

The manuscript consists of two lists, one containing 156 names, the other 2,545. The first list is headed as follows:

These are the people who are of the commune of Provins and who wish to remain there under the government of the mayors and judges [échevins].

The second list is headed as follows:

These are the names of the persons residing in the city of Provins and in the villages belonging to the commune of Provins, who are of the said commune and who wish to be independent and free of the government of the mayors and judges, and who wish to be governed by the king alone.

[71] From F. Bourquelot, *"Un scrutin du XIVe siècle," Mémoires de la société nationale des antiquaires de France,* vol. XXI (1852), pp. 455 ff. For further details concerning this plebiscite, see p. 37 of the historical introduction.

VI TREATIES AND REGIONAL CONSTITUTIONS

— Document No. 42 —

RELATIONS OF SIENA WITH THE RURAL NOBILITY, 1156-1179 [72]

A. 1156. POGGIBONSI. SIENA AND THE COUNT OF TUSCANY

I, Guido Guerra, Count of Tuscany, acknowledge for myself and for my heirs to you, the consuls Ugolino Boste, Malagallie Ariveri, Donosdeo Villani, to your successors, and to the entire people of Siena, that we do not have the authority to sell or place in pledge our share of the hill and castle known as Bonizi to any Florentine, nor may we sell or pledge to them any of our rights, nor indeed to any person without your consent, under penalty of 1000 marcs of silver.

B. 1179. MULIGNANO. MUTUAL OÁTHS OF THE CONSULS OF SIENA AND THE COUNTS OF ARDENGESCA

I swear that I shall uphold the people of all the courts of Ardengesca, that is to say . . . and the people of the others who swore to me earlier; and I promise to support their men, property and allies unless these be openly hostile . . . and I shall protect them in all disputes and wars which they are engaged in now or may be engaged in against all men. I exempt the emperor . . . and all those bound by oath to me; and I promise to them as many men as they may promise to me, and 500 footsoldiers on the

[72] From *Regestum Senese,* ed. Feodor Schneider (Rome, 1908), vol. I, p. 80.

kalends of January. I shall not take any territory in the area of Orgia without the permission of its count or his deputy. And I shall firmly maintain this peace with all the good men of Ardengesca. Should I transgress this oath in any way, I shall make amends within 40 days of my notification by the counts of Ardengesca either in person or in writing.

I shall aid the people of Siena and those allied to them unless these be openly hostile to me, against all men with the exception of the emperor. . . . Within [an area is described] this area, I shall not build or rebuild any castle or fortress save Rocca de Gonfienti, which I may rebuild, and also Rocca de Montepiscine, should it be destroyed. And should I build a castle between the Farma and Lornata rivers, the Sienese people will be free of their oath to me.

— Document No. 43 —

FROM THE PEACE BETWEEN MARSEILLE AND NICE, 1219 [73]

In the name of our Lord, Jesus Christ, the year of the incarnation 1219, fifth indiction, sixth of the kalends of September. It is in the name of Jesus Christ that we fulfill our hopes and succeed in our designs, for it is through Him that we have won the freedom of our city and have built our republic. It is to Him that we owe the development of the laws and advantages of our city; and to Him that we owe the Peace which, with His aid, we shall

[73] From Louis Mery and F. Guindon, *Histoire . . . des actes et des déliberations du corps et du conseil de la municipalité de Marseille depuis le Xe siècle jusqu'à nos jours* (2 vols., Marseille, 1841-43), vol. I, pp. 26-27. Selections.

preserve into the future. It is God alone, Himself, who governs our city.

Concerned with the prospects of our fair city and wishing to provide for its future, the council of our commune composed of the councillors and principal citizens assembles at the sound of the bell . . . [with] deputies especially chosen and empowered by the council and commune of Nice and its district. We declare our agreement and that we have together composed a peace and perpetual harmony in the name of the above-named cities, their inhabitants, and the citizens of their suburbs. By the terms of this concord all the men of Nice and its region, citizens or not, can with perfect freedom live in Marseille and travel to and from the city and its area by land or sea; and this freedom also holds for all the lands where the citizens of Marseille have power over property and life. The people of Nice will live in safety among the men of Marseille and its suburbs and among all peoples over whom the city holds sway. . . .

— Document No. 44 —

THE ESTABLISHMENT OF THE RHINE LEAGUE AND OF ITS PEACE, 1254 [74]

In the name of the holy and undivided Trinity. The judges, consuls [aldermen], and all the citizens of Mainz, Cologne, Worms, Speyer, Strassburg, Basel, and other

[74] From Altmann and Bernheim, *Ausgewahlte Urkunden* (Berlin, 1904), translated in *A Source Book for Medieval History* by Oliver J. Thatcher and Edgar Holmes McNeal, copyright 1905 by Charles Scribner's Sons, 1933 by Oliver J. Thatcher. Reprinted with the permission of the publisher.

cities which are bound together in the league of holy peace, to all the faithful of Christ, greeting in him who is the author of peace and the ground of salvation. 1. Since now for a long time many of our citizens have been completely ruined by the violence and wrongs which have been inflicted on them in the country and along the roads, and through their ruin others have also been ruined, so that innocent people, through no fault of their own, have suffered great loss, it is high time that some way be found for preventing such violence, and for restoring peace in all our lands in an equitable manner.

2. Therefore we wish to inform all that, with the aid of our Lord Jesus Christ, the author and lover of peace, and for the purpose of fostering peace and rendering justice, we have all unanimously agreed on the following terms of peace: We have mutually bound ourselves by oath to observe a general peace for ten years from St. Margaret's day [July 13, 1254]. The venerable archbishops, Gerhard of Mainz, Conrad of Cologne, Arnold of Trier, and the bishops, Richard of Worms, Henry of Strassburg, Jacob of Metz, Bertold of Basel, and many counts and nobles of the land have joined us in this oath, and they as well as we have all surrendered the unjust tolls which we have been collecting both by land and water, and we will collect them no longer.

3. This promise shall be kept in such a way that not only the greater ones among us shall have the advantage of this common protection, but all, the small with the great, the secular clergy, monks of every order, laymen, and Jews, shall enjoy this protection and live in the tranquillity of holy peace. If anyone breaks this peace, we will all go against him with all our forces, and compel him to make proper satisfaction.

4. In regard to the quarrels or differences which now exist between members of this peace, or which may hereafter arise, they shall be settled in the following way: Each city and each lord, who are members of this league, shall choose four reliable men and give them full authority to settle all quarrels in an amicable way, or in some legal manner. . . .

— Document No. 45 —

PARLIAMENTARY SUMMONS IN ENGLAND, 1295 [75]

The king to the sheriff of Northamptonshire. Desiring to hold counsel and treat with the earls, barons, and other nobles of our realm, as to provision against the perils which now threaten it, we have ordered them to meet us at Westminster, on the Sunday next following the feast of St. Martin's in the coming winter, to discuss, ordain and do whatever may be necessary to guard against this danger. We therefore firmly enjoin you to have chosen without delay and sent to us at the said day and place two knights from the said county and two citizens from each city of the said county, and two burgesses from each borough, of those more discreet and powerful to achieve: in such wise that the said knights, citizens and burgesses may severally have full and sufficient power, on behalf of themselves and the community of the county, cities and boroughs to do what may then be ordained by the common counsel in the premises; so that the present business may not in any way rest undone through lack of this power. And bring with you the names of the knights, citizens, and burgesses, and this writ. Witness the King at Canterbury, October third.

[75] From C. W. Colby, *Selections from the Sources of English History* (New York, 1911), pp. 88-90.

THE ORDINANCES OF CARDINAL ALBORNOZ FOR THE PAPAL STATES, 1357 [76]

A. The Functions and Official Oath of a Rector of a Province

The provident authority of law, following the sacred canons, and with wholesome consideration for the welfare and prosperity of the provinces and their inhabitants, has decreed that in each province there shall be one executive head (*praeses*) through whom it shall be efficiently governed and the wishes of the provincials be made plain. These provincial rectors have, with good reason, been given full jurisdiction, with the power of the sword and the duty of inquiry into all kinds of cases. Their office, with its supreme power, has been distinguished by provisions of law, by the good will and sufferance of the Roman pontiffs, and also by praiseworthy custom, with a great variety of honors and privileges. While all these are to remain inviolate (except in so far as they have been or may be modified by the Apostolic See in special cases, and excepting the provisions laid down in the present volume which we require to be observed by the provincial rectors) it has seemed best to us to point out especially certain requirements of the rectorial office

[76] Reprinted by permission of the publishers from Ephraim Emerton, *Humanism and Tyranny* (Cambridge, Mass.: Harvard University Press, 1925), pp. 221-24, 226-29, 235-37, 246, 249, 250. Gil Alvarez de Albornoz (d. 1367) reorganized the papal states from 1353 forward, making possible the return of Urban V to Rome in 1362 from Avignon.

which, if passed over in silence, might seem to be disregarded by us.

It is the duty of a good and prudent rector to give his unremitting care to the preservation of peace and order in his province, to govern the same and to hold it in true loyalty and obedience to the Roman Church and to the Roman pontiffs, under whose absolute sovereignty these provinces belong in spiritual as well as temporal affairs. . . .

B. CHARACTER AND CONDUCT OF RECTORS AND THEIR OFFICIALS

Whereas, according to the witness of our laws, to whom much is entrusted, from him a higher degree of honor and dignity is required:

Therefore we ordain and establish that the rector, who has so arduous a function to perform, and the members of his official family, each according to the principles of honorable conduct, shall refrain from all unlawful actions and wicked extortion. They shall not presume to accept anything beyond the regular payment fixed in this present volume, nor shall they receive anything therein prohibited.

And since, as the law declares, the hearts of judges are corrupted by eating and drinking, the officials of the Rector shall not receive gifts of this kind, either in person or through others; neither shall they forcibly compel anyone to sell them grain or wine or other provisions, but they shall buy only what they need and what is freely sold to them at a fair price actually paid to the dealers before the goods are accepted. Except that, in cases where through the ill will or inability of the inhabitants, things necessary to the execution of their office, such as food, lodging or beds, cannot be purchased, they may with due moderation and restraint compel those who have them to sell them or rent them at a fair price.

The rector shall also require his officials to lead honorable and settled lives. He shall not permit them to wander about or to be involved in loose and quarrelsome ways. Nor shall anyone who does not really belong to the staff of the rector or his judges or officials and regularly live with them take the name of such association under false pretenses or under cover thereof oppress the subjects by unlawful exactions.

The members of the official household shall not be natives or citizens or regular inhabitants of the province; for it is not fitting that anyone under pretense of this relation should gain acquaintance or favors by which he might oppress his fellow citizens in any way. We decree also that the rector shall not within one year appoint anyone who is at the time or who has previously been a member of his staff to the position of podestà or vicar or by any other title in a district where the podestà or other magistrate is regularly appointed by the Rector or by the Church. Nor shall such staff members be chosen by anyone for any office in any place of the aforesaid district or elsewhere lest perchance, if they commit unlawful acts and their subjects are afraid to complain, their offenses should go unpunished, and the subjects be unjustly oppressed.

But this prohibition does not apply to castellans or wardens of fortresses and strongholds. To such offices the rector may appoint members of his household or other trustworthy men as may seem best to him.

The aforesaid prohibition applies also upon corresponding terms to the treasurer of each province and to the members of his official family.

We desire also that a certain decree of the Lord Reformator above mentioned [Bertrand of Embrun] [77] be confirmed and strictly enforced, in which he ordered that no person native to the province or having his home or legal residence there should accept gifts of clothing or other things from the rector or the treasurer—and that these officials should not permit such things to be given to them with or without pay. In case of disobedience he ordered that, in addition to the penalty of excommunication they should pay a fine of 100 gold florins *ipso facto*. . . .

C. Concerning the Parliament and the Army

All bishops, prelates, clergymen and monks, cities, corporations and places, podestas, rectors and nobles, upon the written summons of a rector or treasurer or his vicar, shall be required to attend a Parliament as often as may be ordered and according to prescription.

[77] Bertrand (d. 1355) was Bishop of Embrun in 1323-28, cardinal and vice-chancellor from 1338.

Corporations and cities shall be represented by their own delegates and not by any other community or person or by the representative of another community. No person shall disturb the Parliament by word or deed, and we reserve to the judgment of the rector or his special justice to declare such disturbance and to dispose of it.

We decree that each corporation, commune, noble and every other person shall appear mounted or on foot as shall be ordered by the rector . . . under penalty of punishment. . . .

D. Penalties for Forming Confederations, Leagues, or Assemblies

Seeing that assemblies, confederations and leagues made aforetime without permission of the Apostolic See and the rector of the province have been the cause of serious disturbances and have been provocative of wars and are likely to be so in the future, we cancel and dissolve every association, league, agreement, confederation, brotherhood, captaincy, rectorate, oath, promise, obligation, or pledge, under whatever name or pretext it may have been made or in future shall be made between cities or communes, or lesser units, or of one district or person with another, or by mutual agreement between cities or districts or communes and individuals.

And we order that henceforth no city, commune or individual shall presume to take part in any association, league, obligation, confederacy or agreement or pledge or anything of the kind or any unlawful assembly, or to elect or establish any captain or rector or governor or councillor or by whatever other name they may be called, or to have or hold the obligations of any association or league or agreement or membership in any captaincy or rectorate or military expedition or having anything whatsoever to do with any of these things, or to accept any election or appointment of the sort or consent to it or exercise any such office.

E. Penalty for Using the Words Guelf or Ghibelline by Way of Insult

Whereas party divisions in the provinces and territories aforesaid have been the cause of death and loss of property and the source of great danger to soul and body:

Therefore we, in our unremitting solicitude for the peace and safety of these provinces, decree and ordain that henceforth no person of whatever rank or station shall presume to use the name Guelf or Ghibelline or any other party name as a term of reproach or to invent other names which may tend to the formation of parties, under penalty of 15 gold florins.

And no one shall shout "Long Live" any association or any person, save only "Long Live the Church—or its officials!" The offender, besides the penalty for rioting or other crimes shall be fined 100 gold florins, whether during the same riot he shall have shouted once or many times.

F. Penalty for Neglect of Roads and Bridges

Whereas, on account of the wretched state of warfare prevailing in the aforesaid provinces, bridges, fountains, roads and public highways have been abandoned or destroyed and have so remained to the great danger and injury of the inhabitants:

Therefore, for the common good of the inhabitants we ordain that within the next two months each city, commune, stronghold, town or corporation, and each baron, count or noble shall make diligent effort to reconstruct or repair all bridges, fountains, roads or highways intended for public use, where these have been broken down or discontinued and where none have been to build new ones throughout their territories, so that men and animals and vehicles can freely come and go.

Offenders against this decree, whether cities or other corporations or individuals, shall be punished at the discretion of the rector and judges of the province after careful examination of the condition of the place and persons and the nature of the business and they shall be held responsible for full damages thereby caused.

VII BUSINESS AND COMMERCE
Section 1: Gilds and Crafts

— Document No. 47 —

EXCERPTS FROM THE LOMBARD BOOK OF HONORS, 1010-1020[78]

3. As for the nation of the Angles and Saxons, they have come and were wont to come with their merchandise and wares. . . .

4. As for the duke of the Venetians with his Venetians, he is obligated to give every year in the [king's] palace in Pavia fifty pounds of Venetian deniers. . . . This tribute is called pact because [by it] the nation of the Venetians is allowed to buy grain and wine in every port, and to make their purchases in Pavia, and they are not to suffer any annoyance,

6. Likewise the men of Salerno, Gaeta, and Amalfi were accustomed to come to Pavia with abundant merchandise. And they were wont to give to the treasury in the king's palace the fortieth solidus. And to the wife of the treasurer [they gave] individually spices and accessories just as did the Venetians.

8. As for the *ministerium* of the mint of Pavia, there are to be nine noble and wealthy masters above all the other moneyers, who are to supervise and to direct all other moneyers jointly with the master of the treasury, so

[78] From the *Instituta regalia et ministeria camere regum Longobardorum seu honorantie civitatis Papie,* edited by A. Solmi in *L'amministrazione finanziaria del regno Italico,* pp. 21-24, translated in Lopez and Raymond, *Medieval Trade in the Mediterranean World* (New York, 1955), pp. 57-59.

that they never strike deniers inferior to those they have always struck in regard to weight and silver [content] to wit, ten out of twelve. . . .

9. As for the moneyers of Milan, they are to have four noble and wealthy masters, and with the advice of the treasurer in Pavia are to strike Milanese deniers, equally good as Pavian deniers in regard to silver [content] and weight.

13. There are other *ministeria*. All shipmen and boat-men are obligated to furnish two good men as masters under the authority of the treasurer in Pavia. Whenever the king is in Pavia, they themselves are obligated to go with the ships and these two masters are obligated to out-fit two large vessels, one for the king and one for the queen, and to build a house with planks, and to cover it well. . . .

17. And in regard to all these *ministeria* you should know this: that no man is to perform [his functions] un-less he is one of the *ministri*. . . . Nor ought any mer-chant to conclude his business . . . unless he is one of the merchants of Pavia. . . .

— Document No. 48 —

ROYAL GRANT TO THE WEAVERS OF LONDON, 1154-1162 [79]

Henry, by the grace of God, king of England, duke of Normandy and Aquitaine, count of Anjou, to the bishops, justiciars, sheriffs, barons, and all his servants and liege-men of London, greeting. Know that I have granted to the weavers of London to have their gild in London with

[79] From *English Historical Documents, 1042-1189,* edited by D. C. Douglas and G. W. Greenway. Reprinted by permis-sion of Oxford University Press Inc.

all the liberties and customs which they had in the time
of King Henry, my grandfather. Let no one carry on this
occupation unless by their permission, and unless he belong to their gild, within the city, or in Southwark, or
in the other places pertaining to London, other than those
who were wont to do so in the time of King Henry, my
grandfather. Wherefore I will and firmly order that they
shall everywhere legally carry on their business, and that
they shall have all the aforementioned things as well and
peacefully and freely and honourably and entirely as ever
they had them in the time of King Henry, my grandfather; provided always that for this privilege they pay me
each year 2 marks of gold at Michaelmas. And I forbid
anyone to do them injury or insult in respect of this on
pain of 10 pounds forfeiture, Witness: Thomas of Canterbury; Warin fitz Gerold. At Winchester.

— Document No. 49 —

INVITATION TO WEAVERS TO SETTLE IN COURTRAI, 1224 [80]

I, Jean, Countess of Flanders and Hainault, wish it to
be known to all men living and to be born that I and my
successors will not demand any tallage or tax from such
50 wool weavers as may come to Courtrai from this day
forward. And this shall hold true as long as they live. But
their heirs shall serve me as do my other townsmen.

Courtrai, A.D. 1224, on St. Cecilia's Day

[80] From Espinas and Pirenne, *Recueil des documents rélatifs
à l'histoire de l'industrie drapière en Flandre*, vol. I, pp.
648-49.

— Document No. 50 —

STATUTES ON CLOTHMAKING IN TOULOUSE[81]

When to the presence of the consuls of Toulouse a great multitude of worthy men both of the city and suburb of Toulouse acceded, showing and testifying to the consuls that there were great, many, and diverse dissensions between the worthy drapers, weavers, carders, and finishers of woolen cloth by which the *universitas* of the city and suburb of Toulouse many times sustained fraud and damage, and humbly praying that the said consuls, as they are charged with the common utility, should impose and lend their counsel in this matter:

Therefore, the consuls of the city and suburb of Toulouse, having convoked many experts, and having likewise deliberated greatly in general council with many sound authorities, drapers, weavers, and many others, enacted and issued an ordinance that shall be held and observed incorruptibly in perpetuity, ordaining that. . . .

. . . all weavers may work at their profession day and night wherever it pleases them in the city and suburb. . . . Moreover, these weavers may sell at cheap price as it pleases them. . . .

. . . all apprentices who complete their residence with master weavers may work in their profession in their workshops or in other places with other men and women who manufacture cloth . . . wherever it pleases them, with only the stipulation that they do their work right honestly and well. . . .

. . . all men and women who make cloth or cause it

[81] Sister Mary Ambrose, "Statutes on Clothmaking," *Essays in Medieval Life and Thought*, ed. Mundy, Emery, Nelson (New York, 1955), pp. 172-80.

to be made in their homes are able to hire and keep weavers, nobody resisting, so long as they have contracted with these weavers. Other weavers may not prevent this. . . .

. . . all weavers who have contracted to weave wool should go to weigh the yarn in the homes of him or her from whom they receive the yarn to be woven or in any other place pleasing to the lords or ladies of the yarn. . . .[82]

. . . In each year four worthy men, two from the city and two from the suburb, shall be installed as guardians over the whole woolens profession . . . which four good men, on the same day or the day after the consuls are elected, shall be installed by the elected consuls for the yearly term of the consulate. . . .

This all, as expressed above, [the consuls] ordained and adjudged in a Public Parliament at the Villeneuve Gate.

— Document No. 51 —

A LAW AGAINST STRIKES, 1245 [83]

No one shall be so bold in this city, alone or in company, male or female of the servant class, to start a strike. And should anyone attempt this, he will be fined 60 pounds and be banished a year from the city. . . . And if anyone should foment public agitation against the city, he will be subject to the same penalty, no matter what his trade may be.

1245, January, Douai

[82] The type of contract here described is technically called a *collocatio*. In it, a *dominus* or *domina* provided the raw material and the artisan wove and prepared it. It is interesting to note that landlords and tenants made use of a similar contractual form.

[83] Espinas and Pirenne, *Recueil des documents rélatifs à l'histoire de l'industrie drapière en Flandre*, vol. II, p. 22.

— Document No. 52 —

TROUBLE WITH THE JOURNEYMEN OF THE CORDWAINERS OF LONDON, 1387 [84]

John Clerk, Henry Duntone, and John Hychene, were attached on the 17th day of August, in the 11th year etc., at the suit of Robert de York, Thomas Bryel, Thomas Gloucestre, and William Midenhale, overseers of the trade of Cordwainers, and other reputable men of the same trade, appearing before Nicholas Extone, Mayor, and the Aldermen, in the chamber of the Guildhall of London; and were charged by the said prosecutors, for that— whereas it was enacted and proclaimed in the said city, on behalf of our lord the King, that no person should make congregations, alliances or (compacts) of the people, privily or openly; and that those belonging to the trades, more than other men, should not, without leave of the Mayor, make alliances, confederacies or conspiracies— the aforesaid . . . serving-men of the said trade of Cord-wainers, together with other their accomplices, on the Feast of the Assumption of the Blessed Virgin (15 August) last past, at the Friars Preachers in the said city, brought together a great congregation of men like unto themselves, and there did conspire and confederate to hold together; to the damage of the commonalty, and the prejudice of the trade before mentioned, and in re-bellion against the overseers aforesaid; and there, because that Richard Bonet, of the trade aforesaid, would not agree with them, made assault upon him, so that he hardly escaped with his life; to the great disturbance of the peace of our Lord the King, and to the alarm of the neighbors

[84] From H. T. Riley, *Memorials of London* (London, 1868), p. 495, as quoted in G. G. Coulton, *Social Life in Britain* (Cambridge, 1919), pp. 362-63.

there, and against the oath by which they had before been bound, not to make such congregations or unions, or sects, for avoiding the dangers resulting therefrom. . . .

— Document No. 53 —

SELECTIONS FROM THE USAGES AND CUSTOMS OF THE GILD OF THE HOLY TRINITY OF LYNN, LATE FOURTEENTH CENTURY[85]

If any of the aforesaid bretheren shall die in the said town or elsewhere, as soon as knowledge thereof shall come to the alderman, the said alderman shall order solemn mass to be celebrated for him, at which every brother of the said gild that is in town shall make his offering; and further, the alderman shall cause every chaplain of the said gild, immediately on the death of any brother, to say thirty masses for the deceased.

The alderman and skevins of the said gild are by duty obliged to visit four times a year all the infirm, all that are in want, need, or poverty, and to minister to and relieve all such, out of the alms of the said gild.

If any brother shall become poor and needy, he shall be supported in food and clothing, according to his exigency, out of the profits of the lands and tenements, goods and chattels of the said gild.

No born serf or one of such like condition, nor any apprentice can be received, and if any one of such like condition should be received into the said gild, the alder-

[85] E. P. Cheyney, *Translations and Reprints from the Original Sources of European History* (Philadelphia, n.d.), vol. II, pp. 19-20.

man and his bretheren not knowing it, when it is truly and lawfully proved, such a one shall lose the benefit of the gild.

Section 2: Credit and Usury

— Document No. 54 —

EXAMPLES OF EARLY PUBLIC FINANCE, 1191-1192 [86]

1191

Geradus Caponus, Podestà of the people of Lagneto and Celasco, and Albertus de Lagneto, Jocaremus, Wilhelmus Gota, Oddo, son of Rainerius, and Leonus, son of the now deceased Gandulf, recognize a debt of 10 pounds to Wilhelmus Zetapane. Therefore they give to him and grant in pledge the tolls which they have over the citizens of Lucca. He will collect and hold such tolls for a year beginning next Easter . . . to the extent of 10 pounds. And should there be anything in excess of this figure, he will return it to the Podestà of Lagneto, keeping for himself one-eighth in payment for his services as collector. Done under the arch of the bakers [in Genoa] this very day. Likewise, the aforementioned acknowledge that the commune of Lagneto has received 30 *mezzarolas* of wine from Wilhelmus Zetapane. And they promise to repay this wine from the next vintage according to the judgment of the priests. . . . If the judges should say less, then they will give less [to Zetapane]; and if they say more, the debtors agree to return more. Both the quality of the wine and the quality of the returned containers shall be the same [as that given] under double penalty.

[86] *Guglielmo Cassinese* (*1190-1192*), ed. M. W. Hall, H. C. Krueger, and R. L. Reynolds (Turin, 1938), vol. II, pp. 191-92.

1192

Enricus Papalardus, consul of Savona, promises that
he will give to Petrus de Porta 88 pounds in return for
pepper, the debt to be met the middle of next August,
under threat of double penalty. He swears to pay as speci-
fied above, and swears that he has the consent of his
fellow consuls for the oath he has sworn upon their
souls. . . .

— Document No. 55 —

DECISION OF AN EPISCOPAL COURT ON USURY AT TOULOUSE, 1215 [87]

Be it known to all present and future that Raymond
Augier was summoned for his brother Adhemar Augier
before us, namely Master Pons, Archdeacon of Villemur
and Peter Donati, judges constituted for hearing quarrels
and controversies about usury by the venerable lord Fulk,
Bishop of Toulouse, concerning their suit with the prior
of the Hospital.

The oath of calumny having been taken by both parties, the said Raymond Augier testified that Pons David
had extorted 60 shillings of Toulouse on a debt of 300
shillings contracted by a knight named Bouson, for which
debt Adhemar Augier has stood as surety. And, because
the said prior of the Hospital had inherited the properties
of the said Pons David, now deceased, Raymond Augier
wished and required that the prior answer to the aforesaid
complaint. To this, the attorney appointed by the prior
answered that restitution had been made. Raymond Augier denied that this was so, testifying that mention had
been made of payment which, however, had not been ef-

[87] From J. H. Mundy, *Liberty and Political Power in Toulouse*
(New York, 1954), pp. 208-09.

fected. He further claimed that quittance was made in name only and that it had been recorded by the public notary Bernard of Puysiuran at the will of both parties. Bernard of Puysiuran then testified that the said payment had simply not been made.

And when the attorney of the Hospital admitted that the said money, namely 60 shillings of Toulouse, had been paid as usury, we, namely Master Pons . . . and Peter Donati . . . condemned the attorney of the said Hospital to pay Raymond Augier the said 60 shillings from the properties of the deceased Pons David, . . . ordering and adjudging that the money be paid by the coming feast of St. Sernin, and imposing a penalty in this decision that, unless it be satisfactorily paid by the end of that time, the said attorney for the Hospital shall be required to pay Raymond Augier 12 pennies per week from the goods of Pons David. . . .

— Document No. 56 —

PROVENÇAL STATUTE AGAINST USURERS AND THE CRIME OF USURY, 1235 [88]

It is decreed and established that if anyone should take greater usury than 4 for 5 at the beginning of the year he shall be punished according to the wishes of the court. Nor can usury be demanded on the basis of a concession made by the court. Likewise, it is decreed and established that no usury shall be taken in the sale of any good; and should anyone presume to do this, he shall be punished at the discretion of the court. Likewise it is decreed that the satisfaction of any debt bearing interest shall not be pressed upon any debtor from now until the feast of St. Michael. What is said here of the crime holds with special emphasis with respect to the sale of bread.

[88] From Ch. Giraud, *Essai sur l'histoire du droit français au moyen-âge,* vol. II, p. 15.

Section 3: Commerce and Trade

— Document No. 57 —

SHARES OF A GENOESE SHIP GIVEN IN *COMMENDA*, 1191 [89]

Guglielmo Visconte acknowledges that he has in *accomendatio* from Guglielmo Malfiliastro four shares (*loca*) less one quarter [of a share] of a nef. And the [entire] nef is reckoned at forty shares, and it is the nef which Ugo de Figar and the same Guglielmo sailed from Gaeta to Marseille. And with these shares he can do business and sell and do whatever will seem best to him for the purpose of business. On his return to Genoa he promises to replace in the power of Malfiliastro or of his accredited messenger the profit which God may grant in addition to the capital.

— Document No. 58 —

TESTAMENTARY CREATION OF A SOCIETY FOR THE BENEFIT OF A MINOR, 1218 [90]

[89] R. S. Lopez and I. W. Raymond, *Medieval Trade in the Mediterranean World*, pp. 181-2.

[90] From the Departmental Archives, Haute-Garonne, Order of Malta, Commandery of Toulouse, Bundle 1, Piece 105, dated February 1218.

Item, I, William Raymond, give and dispose to my son Bernard 1,000 shillings of Toulouse which he will put and place in a society with William Hugo and his brother Raymond. Further, William Hugo and his brother will put and place in the said society all the money they may have. This society will continue for seven years, in such a way that all gain made with the aforesaid monies shall be divided in half, so that Bernard will have half and William Hugo and his brother Raymond, the other half. And I, William Raymond, further wish and decree that the said William Hugo be the holder and agent (*tenens et potens*) of the said 1,000 shillings until the end of seven years. And I further wish and decree that my son Bernard and William Hugo and his brother render accounts each year together before my trustees at their summons. And if they learn that the society is not being well directed, William Hugo should be held to make up my son's money to my trustees at their discretion.

— Document No. 59 —

MARKET FOR THE STAPLE OF WOOL, 1319[91]

London. Whereas our lord the King, by writ has signified to us that in particular in his Parliament last holden at York debate was raised touching the establishment of certain places within his realm whereat sales and purchases of wools should be made and not elsewhere; which business (which should turn to the profit of our said lord and of the people of his realm) and also the fixing of the places most convenient herefor, through certain disturbances, remained undetermined; and signified also that divers moneys counterfeiting the coin of our said lord are brought by foreign people into his realm to the subversion of his money, and to the prejudice of our said lord; whereon our lord the King wishes to have our ad-

[91] From A. E. Bland, P. A. Brown, R. H. Hawney, *English Economic History, Select Documents* (London, 1925), pp. 180-81.

vice and counsel; we do him to wit that in full treaty
and discussion with divers merchants citizens, and burgesses of the realm, we have agreed, that if it please our
lord the King, that there be two places established for the
said sales and purchases, namely, one on this side Trent,
and another beyond, which places should fulfil the conditions below-written, that is to say, the places should be
strong, well situated and secure for the repair of foreign
merchants and the safety of their persons and their goods,
and there should be ready access for all manner of merchandise, an exchange good, easy, and prompt, and a
good and convenient haven in the same places; and that
the law and usages and franchises, which merchants re-
pairing to the Staple in these times have had and used,
they should use and enjoy henceforth at the places where
they shall be, without being drawn into another law or
another custom. . . . If it be established in the form
above-written, it will befall to the great profit of our lord
the King and of all his realm; principally, by the security
of the persons and goods of merchants and other people
of the realm . . . and also by the increase of the profit
of the change of our lord through the plate and bullion
which shall be brought there; and also by the drawing of
all manner of merchants and their merchandise that shall
come there. . . .

— Document No. 60 —

ON THE GERMAN *FONDACO* IN VENICE, 1383 [92]

. . . As Philip Gross of Nuremberg, merchant in our
fondaco of the Teutons, relates, he is wont to transport
and to have transported large quantities of wool to the
territory of Lombardy, [acting] for himself and his *socie-
tas*. For these he obtains by way of barter Lombard cloth
which he has transported to Venice. And this would re-

[92] Lopez and Raymond, *Medieval Trade in the Mediterranean
     World*, pp. 85-86.

sult in great profit to the tolls of our Commune and to the advantage of our merchant citizens and of Philip himself if only he were assisted by this special privilege—that whenever he brings or causes to be brought [to Venice] the cloth which he has obtained [in exchange] for the said wool, and after [the cloth] has been duly presented and marked and registered item by item by our *vicedomini,* he be permitted to remove that cloth from the *fondaco* and to put it in a store in Rialto, which has a window, with the purpose of exhibiting the cloth and of selling it as best he can, paying to our Commune the tolls established for the said cloth. And our Commune itself would obtain great advantage from this, since in our *fondaco* there is no place with a window to exhibit the cloth, and furthermore the merchants do not believe that fine cloth should be brought to the *fondaco.* And therefore, [Philip] respectfully has supplicated our government that, considering the aforesaid facts, we should be good enough to concede to him as a special favor that after he brings or causes to be brought to Venice to our *fondaco* some of the said cloth, and after [the cloth] has been presented to and registered by our *vicedomini* and marked by them, and the established toll has been paid, he be allowed to remove it from the *fondaco* and put it in a store in Rialto, which has a window, with the purpose of exhibiting and of selling the cloth just as he would do in the *fondaco.* And for the present, in order that your government may see clearly that the request of the said Philip is just and useful to our Commune and merchants, he would be content to have this favor granted to him for one year, more or less, just as it pleases your government. . . .

BIBLIOGRAPHY

Titles available in English:

The Cambridge Economic History of Europe. Vols. I and
II. Cambridge, 1941-1952.
Clarke, M. V. *The Medieval City State. London,* 1926.

Maine, H. S. *Ancient Law*. London, 1926.

Nelson, B. N. *The Idea of Usury*. Princeton, 1949.

Pirenne, Henri. *Medieval Cities*. Princeton, 1949.

————. *Belgian Democracy*. Manchester, 1915.

Roover, Raymond de. *Money, Banking, and Credit in Mediaeval Bruges*. Cambridge, Mass., 1948.

Rostovtzeff, M. I. *The Social and Economic History of the Roman Empire*. Oxford, 1926.

Stephenson, Carl. *Borough and Town*. Cambridge, Mass., 1933.

Titles available only in foreign languages:

Braudel, Fernand. *La Méditerranée et le monde méditerranéen à l'époque de Philippe II*. Paris, 1949.

Coornaert, Emile. *Les corporations en France avant 1789*. Paris, 1941.

Dahm, Georg. *Untersuchungen zur Verfassungs- und Strafrechtsgeschichte der italienischen Stadt im Mittelalter*. Hamburg, 1941.

Dopsch, Alfons. *Beiträge zur Social- und Wirtschaftsgeschichte*. Vienna, 1938.

Duby, Georges. *La société aux XIe et XIIe siècles dans la région mâconnaise*. Paris, 1953.

Ennen, Edith. *Frühgeschichte der europäischen Stadt*. Bonn, 1953.

Ercole, Francesco. *Dal comune al principato*. Florence, 1929.

Espinas, Georges. *Les origines du capitalism*. 4 vols. Paris, 1933-1949.

Ganshof, F. L. *Étude sur le développement des villes entre Loire et Rhin au moyen âge*. Paris and Brussels, 1943.

Goetz, Walter. *Die Entstehung der italienischen Kommunen im frühen Mittelalter*. Munich, 1944.

Grand, Roger. *Les "Paix" d'Aurillac*. Paris, 1945.

Latouche, Robert. *Les origines de l'economie occidentale*. Paris, 1956.

Lavedan, Pierre. *Histoire de l'urbanisme*. 3 vols. Paris, 1926-1952.

Lestocquoy, J. *Les villes de Flandre et d'Italie sous le gouvernement des patriciens*. Paris, 1952.

Mickwitz, Gunnar. *Die Kartellfunktion der Zünfte und ihre Bedeutung bei Entstehung des Zunftwesens*. Helsinki, 1936.

Niccolai, Franco. *Città e signori*. Bologna, 1941.

Ottokar, Nicola. *Le città francesi nel medio evo*. Florence, 1927.

Petit-Dutaillis, Charles. *Les communes françaises*. Paris, 1947.

Planitz, Hans. *Die deutsche Stadt im Mittelalter*. Graz and Cologne, 1954.

Plesner, Johan. *L'émigration de la campagne a la ville libre de Florence XIIIe siècle*. Copenhagen, 1934.

Rorig, Fritz. *Die europäische Stadt im Mittelalter*. Gottingen, 1955.

Salvemini, Gaetano. *Magnati e populani in Firenze*. Florence, 1899.

Salzer, Ernst. *Über die Anfänge de Signorie in Oberitalien*. Berlin, 1900.

Sánchez-Albornoz y Menduiña, Claudio. *Ruina y extinción del municipio Romano en España e instituciones que le reemplazan*. Buenos Aires, 1943.

Vergottini, Giovanni de. *Arti e popolo nella prima metà del seçolo XIII*. Milan, 1943.

Violante, Cinzio. *La società Milanese nell'età precomunale*. Bari, 1953.

Weber, Max. "Zur Geschichte der Handelsgesellschaften im Mittelalter," *Gesammelte Aufsätze zur Sozial- und Wirtschaftsgeschichte*. Tubingen, 1924, pp. 312 ff.

Wolf, Heinrich. *Volkssouveränität und Diktatur in den italienischen Stadt-republiken*. Leipzig, 1937.

INDEX

VAN NOSTRAND REINHOLD ANVIL BOOKS